"Writing with the careful insights and in
academic, Gary Burge offers wise counsel and sage advice for those who serve in the academic community. Framing the various aspects and stages of an academic career in terms of security, success and significance, Burge applicably, sensitively and skillfully guides the reader through this pilgrimage in a most helpful manner. *Mapping Your Academic Career* should be required reading for all new faculty development programs. Morever, this highly reflective and valuable work deserves a wide readership among those who have been teaching for many years, as well as administrators and board members alike."

David S. Dockery, president, Trinity International University

"I experienced the blessing of team teaching with Gary Burge at Wheaton College for several years. Like his teaching, *Mapping Your Academic Career* is filled with wisdom, insight and the sort of interdisciplinary courage that makes scholars grow and prosper. This book will be a treasure to faculty members at any stage of their academic careers."

Mark R. McMinn, professor of psychology, George Fox University

"Gary Burge aptly applies classic theories of psychological development to the experiences of faculty across the career path. With the turn of each new page, Gary unveiled both my fears and hopes as a junior faculty member. This book inspires self-examination and emotional growth as a means to a meaningful career. *Mapping Your Academic Career* would be an invaluable addition to any orientation program for new faculty."

Elisha Eveleigh, assistant professor of psychology, Wheaton College

"Gary Burge proves himself to be a faculty sage with these wise, perceptive and practical words for faculty at every career stage, and for those who work with them."

Joel B. Green, dean of the School of Theology, Fuller Theological Seminary

"This book is wonderfully humane: *humane* because it does not say what a generic faculty member should look like, but instead carefully considers the developmental stages that take place in a professor's life; *wonderful* because Burge's book is brimming with deep insights, helpful anecdotes and wise counsel. His vision for faculty mentoring could especially yield great fruit for all who will follow it. Highly recommended to administrators and faculty alike."

Kelly M. Kapic, professor of theological studies, Covenant College

"Professor Burge has offered the academic community an exquisite gift: a guide to those called into the teaching vocation within higher education. It is a handbook of sorts—a resource for faculty at each stage of their careers so that they can effectively steward their lives and the work to which they are called. The book reflects a theological vision for this good work and is also eminently practical, with timely advice for young, middle-aged and older faculty."

Gordon T. Smith, president, professor of systematic and spiritual theology, Ambrose University

"Gary Burge, in his book *Mapping Your Academic Career,* brings needed wisdom for those who are on lifelong journeys as academics. He draws on the insights of developmental psychology but grounds it in an understanding of the practice of spiritual disciplines in order to assist independent-minded academics in navigating the ongoing tensions of working within the constraints of an institutional mission, while being on their own life journey of identity formation."

Janel Curry, provost, Gordon College

Mapping Your Academic Career

Charting the Course
of a Professor's Life

Gary M. Burge

IVP Academic

An imprint of InterVarsity Press
Downers Grove, Illinois

InterVarsity Press
P.O. Box 1400, Downers Grove, IL 60515-1426
ivpress.com
email@ivpress.com

InterVarsity Press® is the book-publishing division of InterVarsity Christian Fellowship/USA®, a
movement of students and faculty active on campus at hundreds of universities, colleges and schools of
nursing in the United States of America, and a member movement of the International Fellowship of
Evangelical Students. For information about local and regional activities, visit intervarsity.org.

All Scripture quotations, unless otherwise indicated, are taken from THE HOLY BIBLE, NEW
INTERNATIONAL VERSION®, NIV® Copyright © 1973, 1978, 1984, 2011 by Biblica, Inc.™ Used by
permission. All rights reserved worldwide.

While any stories in this book are true, some names and identifying information may have been changed
to protect the privacy of individuals.

Cover design: Cindy Kiple
Interior design: Beth McGill
Images: old books: © dem10/iStockphoto
        sailboat illustration: © debela/iStockphoto

ISBN 978-0-8308-2473-1 (print)
ISBN 978-0-8308-9857-2 (digital)

Printed in the United States of America ∞

InterVarsity Press is committed to ecological stewardship and to the conservation of natural resources in
all our operations. This book was printed using sustainably sourced paper.

Library of Congress Cataloging-in-Publication Data

Burge, Gary M., 1952-
  Mapping your academic career : charting the course of a professor's life / Gary M. Burge.
      pages cm
  Includes bibliographical references and index.
  ISBN 978-0-8308-2473-1 (pbk. : alk. paper)
  1. College teachers—Vocational guidance—United States. 2. Learning and scholarship—United States. I.
Title.
  LB1778.2.B87 2015
  378.1'2023—dc23
                                                                                    2015014881

P   22   21   20   19   18   17   16   15   14   13   12   11   10   9   8   7   6   5   4

Y   36   35   34   33   32   31   30   29   28   27   26   25   24   23   22

For my many colleagues past and present who

have wisely interpreted and modeled

our academic career.

CONTENTS

PREFACE

I have always imagined this short book as a conversation—a conversation I wish I had had almost thirty years ago when I first began working as a college professor. Life in the academy is a peculiar trade: we complete our terminal degrees (usually a PhD), find a generous employer who will take a risk on our unproven skills, and suddenly, there we are standing before thirty or forty students between the ages of eighteen and twenty-one. But unlike most trades, our preparation in graduate school did not train us to do what we do most. We may excel at research, but we spend a tremendous amount of time managing the classroom, student relationships, lecturing and grading. Not to mention committees and general college life. And no one prepared us for any of it. I used to think about that hour in the classroom as the delivery of tightly organized information, a style not unlike the defense of a thesis or the presentation of an academic paper. Today I wouldn't imagine doing such a thing.

Every trade has secrets. And within every trade there are those who become masters of these mysteries and still others who do not. I have watched the same thing for years: triumph and sorrow, success and failure. While some of those failures were perhaps inevitable, I am convinced that most of them were not. The chief problem is that we are not taught to think reflectively about our own work *as teachers.* Inspiring, valuable essays by writers like Parker Palmer (whose work revolutionized my own teaching) are deeply useful. But few of us think concretely and practically about how we do what we do. I have known famous professors who sustained a PhD-level research trajectory right through their careers. Their books brought them and their college fame. And yet in some cases, they were abysmal teachers. And I wondered, particularly when I was younger: Is this the path to success in the academy?

Moreover, we rarely think about ourselves developmentally. I am a person who is changing every decade, and this reality affects the role I play in my college. It only dawned on me about eight years ago that my relationships with students are evolving and are substantially different today than when I was about thirty-five. Once I figured this out and did some casual reading about development theory, suddenly the fog cleared and I could see the path ahead. And I liked what I saw. *Truth is, I don't want to be the thirty-five-year-old professor again.* Let me cite just one example. Few students are looking for another friendship among faculty. But countless students are desperately looking for what we might call the "trusted older adult." Or as Richard Rohr might call it, "the sage." This is a complex term we'll explore, and although the word itself seems excessive to me, it gets at something important. Unless we understand our place in the natural stages of life and see how we are developing and changing, unless we are truly mindful, we will miss new and rewarding opportunities. But if we do not permit ourselves these new roles—or they are denied to us by others—tragedy and disappointment may well result.

So think of this as a conversation, a private conversation between two professors. It is a conversation I've been thinking about for a long time and one I hope you're willing to have with me.

A number of friends and colleagues have read this manuscript and critiqued it. Others discussed its themes with me at length and helped me refine them. Their input, inspiration and stories are in evidence throughout. Special thanks go to Emily Langan, Elisha Eveleigh, Mike Kibbe, Carol Burge, David Lauber, Gene Green, Leah Anderson, Max Lee, Rich Butman, Jennifer McNutt, Leah Samuelson, Terri Watson, Andrew Hill, Matthew Patton and Jill Baumgaertner. In particular David Lauber (theology) and Rich Butman (psychology) have been conversation partners for many years, and their insight and wisdom have been invaluable. Also, thanks are due to my research assistant, Jessica Cruise, who compiled the index. Daniel Reid at InterVarsity Press not only served as my editor but as my advisor, providing helpful guidance and encouragement. He is a "Cohort 3 Sage."

I have included a number of stories in this book that illustrate the ideas under discussion. In each case I have changed personal details for obvious reasons. But in each case, the essence of what happened is true.

■ ■ ■

Mapping Your Academic Career can be used as a resource for faculty development programs at colleges and universities. Dr. Gary Burge can also be contacted as a speaker for these events. See garyburge.org or email him at gary.burge@wheaton.edu.

Introduction

MAPPING OUR LIVES

My interest in the developmental stages of the academic career was born in the summer of 2007. I found myself in the office of an orthopedic surgeon who was looking at an x-ray pinned to a wall-mounted light table. Then he used a word foreign to my vocabulary: *arthritis*. Arthritis? I *can't* have arthritis—my parents have arthritis. My grandparents had arthritis. He went on: "Actually you have *patellofemoral chondromalacia*. But if you prefer, we also call it 'runner's knee.'" I preferred. My psyche seemed to relax.

Later that same month I received an envelope from the AARP (American Association of Retired Persons) encouraging me to join up. *Join up?* A free copy of *AARP The Magazine* (before 2002, *Modern Maturity*) had Clint Eastwood on the cover. He was born in 1930.

And then a very kind young woman who was about nineteen offered me a "senior discount" at a local golf course. All of a sudden my consciousness was raised (perhaps *alarmed* is a better word) and it forced me to consider the developmental passages I had moved through and whether I was entering a new one.

Frankly, up till this point, I wasn't aware that there were passages at all. It seemed that once you entered adulthood, well, the road was fairly level till you retired. And in a culture that worships youth, in your fifties you do your best to perform like you are an energetic thirty.

Psychology has had a long history of mapping the development of the personality. From Freud's (1886–1939) psychosexual theory, to Jean Piaget's (1896–1980) cognitive development theory, to Erik Erikson's (1902–1994) eight-step psychosocial development model, psychologists have attempted to parse the formative influences that make us what we are and map the stages we travel through in our lives.[1]

The real question posed by Piaget and Erikson that seems to control the discussion is this: are there milestones or competencies that we must achieve in order for us to reach maturity? Piaget suggested four competencies, and in his view, if we do not achieve them we become stuck and our development becomes handicapped. For example, a Piaget model suggests that self-interest and a simplistic worldview must give way to generosity and complexity. However, many remain stuck and stay in their adulthood with features they should have abandoned years earlier. We've each seen faculty members like this.

Erikson disagreed. In his model (with its eight milestones) we carry forward in life each of our developmental failures, and this shapes how we address new questions that life *demands* we answer as we grow. Today Erikson's view is popular. Subsequent writers, however, have added numerous caveats. In Erikson's later adult stages it is *crises* and *the stresses they impose* as well as our adaptive responses to them that will determine our progress. Crises force us to reevaluate our priorities, reorder our lives and prepare for age-related changes that are on the horizon. Most therapists I know think that this aptly describes most of their clients.

The most well-known researcher who examined these critical crisis-driven shifts was Daniel Levinson (1920–1994). Levinson wrote highly

---

[1]For a thorough summary of social and psychological research into adult development in the twentieth century see George Vaillant, *Aging Well: Surprising Guideposts to a Happier Life from the Landmark Harvard Study of Adult Development* (New York: Little/Brown, 2002) pp. 39-82.

influential adult development theories called *The Seasons of a Man's Life* (1978) and *The Seasons of a Woman's Life* (1986). Here he introduced the notion of "midlife crisis"—an idea, incidentally, that has not done well in subsequent study. Nevertheless, the wider notion seems correct: crises can be formative stimuli for change. Levinson believed that we each experience these "crises" in discrete periods of life: in our late twenties or thirties, sometime between forty and fifty, and later as we enter our sixties. These are three stages when certain things begin to slip away from us and other opportunities present themselves. In this spirit, in 1987 Judith Viorst wrote *Necessary Losses: The Loves, Illusions, Dependencies, and Impossible Expectations That All of Us Have to Give Up in Order to Grow,* and she suggested that it is loss—embracing loss—that is a catalyst to our growth.

Richard Rohr (the inspirational Catholic speaker and writer) likes to talk about ascent and descent to typify the grand cycle of our lives. According to Rohr, unless we understand the limits of ascent and how to embrace descent, our lives will end in tragedy. But this is a difficult assignment, particularly since our society thinks we should be ascending like a rocket every year. A quick look at his most recent book, *Falling Upward: A Spirituality for the Two Halves of Life* (2011), tells it all. We all fall. Aging can be a crisis. But this fall can also be an ascent. And Rohr is eager to tell us how.

A retired professor now in his eighties offered me Paul Tournier's good book *Learn to Grow Old* (1972). I assumed it would have little relevance to anyone under eighty—until Tournier explained that the patterns of our lives that we set *now* in early years determine how we either celebrate or detest the later years of our lives.[2]

Then another friend, a psychologist this time, handed me George Vaillant's remarkable book *Aging Well* (2002). This is the outcome of the longest study on aging ever completed entitled the "Study of Adult Development at Harvard University." Based on three cohorts making up

---

[2]This reminds me of something that St. Ignatius of Loyola was once to have said, "Give me a child till he is seven, and I'll show you the man."

824 people, participants were selected carefully as teenagers in the 1920s and 1930s. They represented three very different social strata in American society and they have been studied carefully throughout their lives (they are now in their 70s and 80s). And in this book we have Vaillant's careful interpretation of these cohorts (chiefly using Freud and Erikson). We can learn that it is possible to *age well* and it is possible to *age poorly* as their many subjects demonstrate. If each of us are aging (and of course we are) then I for one want to discover the keys, the secrets, that facilitate not only a life well lived, but a life that ages well.

In each case, these writers have identified formative influences that bring each of us to maturity (sexual resolution, individuation, socialization, attachment, personal loss, etc.). And from here we consolidate our identities, we test them, we either flourish or fail, and we ready ourselves for decline and mortality. Numerous factors weigh into these results: our genetic history, our gender, how we were parented, birth order, relational crises, family systems, our mother's mental outlook, etc. Not surprisingly, there is often a correlation between personality traits seen early in childhood and traits exhibited in adult life. I sometimes imagine some of the college presidents I've known when they were five years old. I can see them now taking charge of the kindergarten and giving orders on the playground.

I am narrowly interested in adult development stages as they are experienced within the traditional academic career in a college or university. We can find manuals that will tell us the specifics of career success such as *Faculty in New Jobs* (1999), *How to Succeed in Academics* (2000), *Managing Your Academic Career* (2000) or *The Joy of Teaching: A Practical Guide for New College Instructors* (2005).[3] But these do not

---

[3]R. J. Menges, *Faculty in New Jobs: A Guide to Settling In, Becoming Established, and Building Traditional Support* (San Francisco: Jossey-Bass, 1999); L. L. McCabe and E. R. B. McCabe, *How to Succeed in Academics* (San Diego: Academic, 2000); D. Royce Sadler, *Managing Your Academic Career: Strategies for Success* (St. Leonards, NSW: Allen & Unwin, 2000); P. Filene, *The Joy of Teaching: A Practical Guide for New College Instructors* (Chapel Hill: University of North Carolina Press, 2005).

engage how faculty members evolve over their careers.

This developmental approach has witnessed limited attention.[4] One of the first to attempt this was Harold L. Hodgkinson, whose Levinson-inspired 1974 essay, "Adult Development: Implications for Faculty and Administrators," began a conversation that continues today.[5] Although age was a key factor in how he sorted faculty "stages," he warned of its limitations because developmental cycles can vary far outside age parameters among faculty.

In 1982, forty-eight faculty at research universities were carefully studied to see if developmental patterns could be charted in their careers. They could be.[6] Something forms within us at about age thirty. Something else takes place midcareer. And still new developments are shaping us as we reach older senior status. These and other more recent studies share the same interests: What are the formative adult developmental processes that make us who we become? Can they be predicted? Measured? And how do they show up in our professorial careers? If college leaders knew this, they would be well on their way to understanding how to build successful faculty development programs rather than the one-size-fits-all programs we see today. Still, as good as these studies may be, they each share a similar lack. They invest little in the developmental experiences of faculty over fifty.

To address this, in 1981 Roger Baldwin and Robert Blackburn studied select faculty at twelve liberal arts colleges and tried to synthesize observations from studies up till that time.[7] In 1993 a developmental study

---

[4]In what follows, see the summaries in Carole J. Bland and William H. Bergquist, *The Vitality of Senior Faculty Members: Snow on the Roof—Fire in the Furnace* (Washington, DC: George Washington University Graduate School of Education and Human Development, 1997), pp. 39-52.

[5]Harold L. Hodgkinson, "Adult Development: Implications for Faculty and Administrators," *Educational Record* 55, no. 4 (1974): 263-74.

[6]L. A. Braskamp et al., "Faculty Development and Achievement: A Faculty View," paper presented at the 1982 meeting of the American Educational Research Association, New York, 1982.

[7]Roger G. Baldwin and Robert T. Blackburn, "The Academic Career as a Developmental Process," *Journal of Higher Education* 52, no. 6 (1981): 588-614.

was made, but it was limited to the careers of senior faculty.[8] Perhaps the most interesting and certainly only well-known longitudinal study was made by Joseph Axelrod, who published the forty-year history of a disguised, though genuine, faculty member (named Stephen Abbot). In one volume, Abbot is a young professor in his thirties.[9] In the next, we find Abbott in midlife.[10] Later we meet him in his midfifties and sixties.[11] In each study, we see the evolution of his career.

Perhaps the newest collaborative effort to study faculty development and success was launched in 2002 at Harvard's Graduate School of Education. Called the Collaborative on Academic Careers in Higher Education (often called "COACHE"),[12] this is a consortium of over two hundred colleges and universities that is attempting to quantify faculty success in order to learn "best practices" for faculty development. They publish papers, hold conferences and can generate college-specific reports based on surveys (which are then compared with national data). COACHE can even provide on-site visits to give guidance to faculty and administrative leaders in member institutions.

There is a literature devoted to the career preparation of deans and provosts that seeks to chart the relationships they might have with faculty at various stages. But here *tenure* is the main watershed, and questions of promotion, discipline and career development of faculty are foremost. There is also a literature exploring the mission and future of higher education—both secular and confessional—in American society. Religious writers have taken this up directly: Robert Benne's *Quality with Soul* (2001) and Duane Litfin's *Conceiving the*

---

[8]Martin J. Finkelstein and Mark W. LaCelle-Peterson, eds., *Developing Senior Faculty as Teachers* (San Francisco: Jossey-Bass, 1993).

[9]Joseph Axelrod, *The University Teacher as Artist* (San Francisco: Jossey-Bass, 1973).

[10]Joseph Axelrod, "From Counterculture to Counterrevolution: A Teaching Career," in Eble, K., ed., *Improving Teaching Styles.* (San Francisco: Jossey-Bass, 1980).

[11]Joseph Axelrod, "The Case of Stephen Abbot," in Carole J. Bland and William H. Bergquist, eds., *The Vitality of Senior Faculty Members: Snow on the Roof—Fire in the Furnace*, (Washington, DC: George Washington University, 1997) pp. 13-38.

[12]http://isites.harvard.edu/icb/icb.do?keyword=coache&pageid=icb.page307142.

Christian College (2004) come to mind. Here the well-being, and survival of the Christian academy is at stake. Missional fidelity and loss take center stage. Many such books examine in remarkable detail the institutional role of presidents, boards and development officers in that survival.

However, few explore the developmental shifts—the well-being, perhaps—that follow faculty members for the thirty or forty years they work as professors. Richard Hughes attempts to chart the *Vocation of the Christian Scholar* (2005) and asks what elements will keep faculty committed to a richly integrated Christian commitment in their work. But he has limited interest in developmental shifts in our lives.

Occasionally very specific advice lists are printed, such as John Vineyard's "How to Prosper in the 3 Stages of a Campus Career."[13] I was hoping this would be a goldmine of wisdom until I learned that he is a financial manager giving advice to us on how to build an investment portfolio as nontenured, tenured and retired professors. That's hardly my present interest. But more practical tips can be found in the splendid practical journal *The Teaching Professor* (and its helpful website). Here are archived tips for the teacher and ample room for blogging.[14]

But to my knowledge few have tried to map the developmental stages that follow the professorial career and provide practical advice on how to navigate those stages. What would happen, I wondered, if we examined how traditional developmental stages among adults present themselves within this one profession?

My own professional experiences have also made me curious to understand the lives of those with whom I have worked. I began my first faculty position as a young professor in 1982. Since then, I have served in three very different colleges. Each of these has been confes-

---

[13]John Vineyard, "How to Prosper in the 3 Stages of a Campus Career," *The Chronicle of Higher Education*, February 27, 2004.

[14]See www.teachingprofessor.com. Today online access to the archive is by subscription. Many colleges purchase a subscription for the entire faculty.

sionally Christian; however, each understood the integration of that confession differently. For one, it was a casual commitment and in some respect it was not always apparent that the college deemed its religious identity as central. At another college, faculty openly criticized the religious mission of the school, much to the dismay of denominational leaders who, frankly, were eager to reorient the faculty as soon as possible. For my present college it is a serious and intentional commitment that sometimes creates anxiety among faculty who hope they actually "fit in." Chapel is required for students three times each week, faculty are expected to mentor students spiritually, and doctrinal interests are very much a part of the faculty hiring process.

Now almost thirty years have passed, and while all of it has been rewarding, there were many times when I wished someone had tipped me off regarding those things that would have helped me flourish and what things might be lethal to a fledgling career. I sometimes feel like I possess an archive of memories and can call up countless stories of people who have succeeded; and I can think of many others who have, in some respects, failed.

Every developmental theory is personal, and this is as true of Levinson as it is of me. My own view certainly owes a lot to my own place in my career and my society. My age, my gender, my socioeconomic location and my career experiences have each shaped my understanding of how we grow and change. And this leads to a fair question: Can these observations be generalized? For instance, being a man in the academy brings certain realities quite different than what a woman may experience. My hope is that this paradigm is sufficiently wide and flexible that others different from who I am may find something here of use.

THE THREE COHORTS OF THE PROFESSORIAL CAREER

Adult careers are often divided in threes. This is the model that Levinson suggested, and it has much to commend it. John Vineyard writes, "For an artisan, the trinity might be apprenticeship, competency and mastery. For someone in business, it might be junior executive, senior executive and CEO. For an academic, it might be tenure track, post-tenure and retirement. The permutations are endless."[15] The usual divisions are (1) career learning, (2) career mastery and (3) career completion or retirement. In my experience, however, this oversimplifies what we experience as college professors and neglects more subtle divisions within the academy.

I believe that we enter three discrete "cohorts" *before retirement* as we move through our careers.[16] These cohorts have no relationship to the traditional three academic titles regularly used (assistant professor, associate professor, full professor). Instead they reflect a person's *perception* of one's relationship to oneself, one's career and the college one serves. They may also measure the college's perception of how a faculty member is progressing and is valued as shown by recognition, task assignments, grants and promotion. There are cases where faculty with fifteen years of experience still see themselves as junior and are in some manner developmentally stuck. And there are other faculty who within a year or two exhibit a sense of largesse and entitlement that you generally only see among tenured professors in their sixties.

I am not a psychotherapist. But thanks to the coaching of many therapists around me and my long participation in our college's doctoral psychology program,[17] I have been able to listen in to their conversations, learn some of the vocabulary of this discipline and think about it as I look back on almost thirty years as a college professor. I have watched many, many colleagues do well—and others do poorly. I have seen many manage career thresholds with courage and resolve;

---

[15]Vineyard, "How to Prosper."

[16]Baldwin and Blackburn, "The Academic Career," suggest five stages: (1) assistant professors in their first three years, (2) assistant professors with three years experience, (3) associate professors, (4) full professors with more than five years before retirement, (5) full professors within five years of retirement.

[17]I team-teach the PsyD capstone seminar with a psychologist each year in Wheaton College's Graduate School of Psychology.

others were filled with dismay and confusion. Some have ended their careers with great satisfaction; still others ended with profound despair and, in a few cases, relief that "it all is over." Two friends I know retired about fifteen years ago. One friend valued his teaching career and yet looked forward to the new horizon with healthy anticipation. He had splendid plans. The other friend's recent words to me were, "I am so glad I left that __ place." And today he seems, well, frustrated. My first friend gave me some sage advice that I've always valued: always listen to people ten years older than you so you know what's coming. That was helpful to me—and it also gave me an insight into how he perceptively viewed his own life.

So what made the difference between these two men? My quest has been to understand the stages of our careers and the transitions that divide them and thereby map how we move across the landscape of the academy.

By now I have discussed these cohorts with dozens of colleagues. And in each case, they have come away from the discussion describing how this accurately represents their experiences. This is particularly true for midcareer and senior faculty who have at least twenty years of experience. They are able to look back over their lives and with discernment think about the turns they made and the beneficial choices that helped them along.

In figure 0.1, three cohorts represent three "stages" of development in a scholar's career. Significant "markers" divide them. Note carefully that these cohorts do not represent faculty rank. These are fluid developmental stages keyed to experience. Note as well that age ranges cannot be fixed. The usual career—when a person completes his or her terminal degree from ages twenty-eight to thirty-two—is my working assumption. However a person might easily be in Cohort 2 at thirty-five or just entering the profession (Cohort 1) at forty. And when a person moves from one college to another, new variables may shift the cohort location. I also suspect that these configurations will shift depending on gender, because many men and women will report very different professional experiences. And the same may be true for ethnicity or culture.

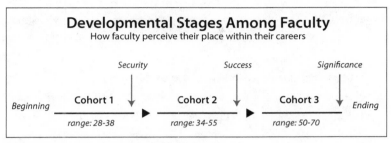

Figure 0.1. Developmental stages among faculty

It is not difficult to observe that faculty change over the years. With understandable frustration, deans have noted something as simple as faculty meeting attendance. Younger faculty attend loyally, and this interest decreases as faculty enter Cohort 3 (see below on what will keep them coming). Of course there are exceptions, but I have yet to find someone who will question the general rule. Interest in committee work also declines as fewer and fewer Cohort 3 faculty will run for elected office—and then they often decline minor committee appointments or service (again, there are always exceptions). Everyone knows the lament: *It seems like junior faculty do all the committee work.* Is this simply indifference or laziness? Or is something important happening within the souls of our senior colleagues? As Kate Sandberg at the University of Alaska has written, perhaps what we need is mentoring programs *for senior faculty* who need to understand themselves better.[18]

Others observe a decline in competitiveness. Cohort 1 faculty have emerged fresh from a graduate program and are often eager to "make a name" for themselves and rise above their peer group. Cohort 3

---

[18]Kate Sandberg, "Senior Professors, Too, Sometimes Need a Helping Hand," *The Chronicle of Higher Education*, March 16, 2001, http://chronicle.com/article/Senior-Professors-Too/4861/.

faculty have a complex set of reactions to competition (as we will see). Some continue to strive; others have given up altogether. Cohort 1 faculty work hard to burnish their reputations among students; Cohort 3 do so less. There is thus a *developmental history* at work here: faculty move through measurable stages of development and evolve. But as they evolve, we will see how they make choices and what the consequences of those choices are.

Perhaps the most persistent observation I discovered is how faculty in these three cohorts view their relationship to the institution they serve. Before I explore this at greater length, let me outline the broad contours. Cohort 1 faculty can view the college as *hovering* over them. This is easily explained through the rigorous assessment that they experience before tenure. Anxiety and fatigue is often their lot. Cohort 2 expresses this relationship as *formative*. This points to the investment and regard they perceive from the college's leadership. They often feel genuinely empowered. Cohort 3 may refer to *invisibility*. This group will often wonder if their role is still noticed and if student evaluations or post-tenure assessments really count for much. As one respected senior colleague put it, "My phone simply stopped ringing."

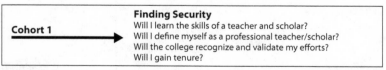

Cohort 1

Finding Security
Will I learn the skills of a teacher and scholar?
Will I define myself as a professional teacher/scholar?
Will the college recognize and validate my efforts?
Will I gain tenure?

Figure 0.2. Cohort 1

In this sense, each cohort has distinct developmental tasks that can be charted. Cohort 1 must locate security and a profound sense of vocational identity. Here the vital developmental issues center on *core identity formation*. The chief institutional goal is to identify risk areas while faculty members establish their professional identity, form successful professional habits and become valued, contributing members of the community. Young faculty tell me how alert they are to these tensions of finding security. Some will describe hidden competitiveness with their recently hired peers. Some will confess jealousy when a colleague is offered a special opportunity and they wonder to themselves, "How did *that person* get invited to do *that*?"

But once security is found, Cohort 2 launches an entirely different set of developmental issues. The question is no longer whether or not the college will retain or promote; the issues now are internal to the professor's own sense of *presence* within his professional community. Now new questions arise.

As we will see, this is a period of matured scholarship and teaching. And this is when institutional investment in the faculty member peaks. Colleges look to this cohort for an enormous contribution in things such as faculty leadership and student mentoring. And in addition, this is where colleges will look for their "heroes" who will contribute to the legacy that the college preserves and protects.

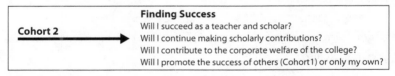

Finding Success
Will I succeed as a teacher and scholar?
Will I continue making scholarly contributions?
Will I contribute to the corporate welfare of the college?
Will I promote the success of others (Cohort 1) or only my own?

Cohort 2

Figure 0.3. Cohort 2

The margin between Cohort 1 and 2 is clear: it is security generally expressed through tenure (or long-term contracts). The margin between Cohort 2 and 3 is far less obvious, and faculty rarely know that this threshold exists. However, when I have explained it to them it immediately registers: new questions are being asked about *core identity*, and they wonder if there is still time for growth and change. Curiously, Cohort 1 and 3 faculty have more in common than they realize.

Cohort 3 can be a time of crisis and self-doubt that generally remains disguised among peers. Or it can be a time of remarkable enrichment and contribution—some say the most rewarding time of their lives. One study of 1,135 senior faculty in six institutions found levels of job satisfaction that were higher than junior faculty (although they also reported that they found the transitions in their career to be increasingly stressful).[19]

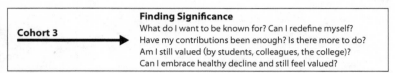

Figure 0.4. Cohort 3

Above all Cohort 3 faculty are asking why they do what they do and whether there is a new venue to practice in. Many question their career path; some think about changing jobs or locales (but they generally conclude that their age makes a major change impossible). If the college leadership does not recognize this cohort and cultivate its possibilities, these faculty may languish.

Therefore each of these cohorts can be distinguished by their possibilities and their risks. It is possible to flourish in any cohort. *But it is also possible to fail in any cohort.* There is a turning point that characterizes each developmental stage.

But here is my most alarming observation. For the most part, scholars in the field of clinical psychology are remarkably self-aware. It is not uncommon to hear the best clinical psychology faculty reflect on their own developmental processes as they move through life. In other words, they see mapping *themselves* as a necessary component to becoming a growing adult. And yet most of us within the academy do not think about our own adult maps. We can analyze any subject and make discerning critiques of writers in our fields (as some may have already critiqued these paragraphs!). And yet the one thing we

[19]R. Armour et al., "Senior Faculty Careers and Personal Development: A Survey," paper presented at the 1989 Annual Meeting of the American Educational Research Association, March 27–31, San Francisco, CA, summarized in Bland and Bergquist, *Vitality of Senior Faculty*, p. 51.

rarely do is reflect on ourselves, what we are feeling about our age or our accomplishments or our aims. Simply put, we often lack *skilled discernment* when we think about life. What some therapists call "mindfulness." In the words of the popular magazine *Psychology Today*,

> Mindfulness is a state of active, open attention on the present. When you're mindful, you observe your thoughts and feelings from a distance, without judging them good or bad. Instead of letting your life pass you by, mindfulness means living in the moment and awakening to experience.[20]

Because of our lack of attentiveness to our inner processes, we mis-identify ourselves with roles that belong to other cohorts and we miss opportunities—rich opportunities—that are sitting right before us.

Don't think that a senior faculty member you know on your faculty has this solved. I certainly do not. And don't make the mistake of thinking that deans or provosts are any different than the rest of us. It is the rare member of the academy in any role who reflects creatively on what it means to evolve as an adult and permits his or her job to evolve as well.

---

[20]*Psychology Today* (January 2013), online: www.psychologytoday.com/basics/mindfulness.

Cohort One

WILL I FIND SECURITY?

I remember well the year I completed my PhD in the United Kingdom. I had just passed my oral examination at Durham University in England, phoned my wife with the good news from a British pay phone (yes, I crammed a pocketful of coins into the phone slot in those days), and headed back to my first college teaching job, which was already underway. That same year a well-known publishing company expressed interest in publishing my dissertation (something that came into reality a year later). I thought I knew the names of all the leading lights in my field; I knew countless other graduate students who were just coming up for jobs; and I had endless ideas for subjects that needed to be explored in print.

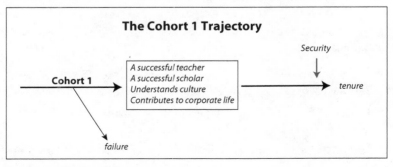

Figure 1.1. The Cohort 1 trajectory

My classes were full; students liked those of us who were younger, and we often wondered if the older faculty really understood the students' world and their needs. They didn't know the music, the films, the clothes. And they were generally so uncool. We were (as one administrator told us) "young bucks" who were as enthusiastic as we were impulsive. We could find a way to improve anything we saw.

Iconoclasts? Indeed. At moments, I am sure we were downright annoying. I am grateful to one very secure, very wise president who knew how to channel our energies before we destroyed the campus or found ourselves shot by some senior faculty member.

Cohort 1 faculty have recently completed their graduate study, and because of this, their research skills are sharp, they know their discipline well, and they have research ideas they would like to pursue. If given the right opportunities early enough, they can sustain the energy level of their PhD research and develop lifelong disciplines of writing and speaking. They are hallmarked by vigor and will tend to energize those environments where they work. And it goes without saying that their age will often enable them to connect with students who may be only ten years younger. These are all advantages, but as we will see, they also come with considerable risks.

FOUR TRAITS OF COHORT 1

The developmental task of Cohort 1 faculty members is to *learn the trade*. In this sense they are traditional apprentices living out all of the anxieties that necessarily come with a new trade. They must learn the skills of good teaching and develop the habits of a lifelong scholar. They must learn the culture in which they work and decide how they are going to fit into the corporate life of the community. Do they heartily embrace that culture (and bond to it) or do they feel strong dissonance (and later experience cynicism)?

The catch for the young professor is that, unlike most disciplines, earning a PhD does not provide instruction in how to do these things.

Consider the different training given to a physician or a surgeon. Their work is inspected by peers regularly—few surgeries are conducted in isolation—and a part of the training involves a directed apprenticeship. The young scholar has no such guidance. Occasionally a department chair or dean may visit a class, but this is announced beforehand so the teaching performance can be perfectly orchestrated. This gives a limited view of the young teacher's consistent ability. It would be like attending a dinner party once every four months and thinking that the menu that night reflected the menus every night of the week.

Therefore, new Cohort 1 members are unskilled and will always make mistakes. And that means they will constantly need reaffirmation, clear feedback and confidence that they can "do over" the things that have not gone well. However, they are effective learners—that is the golden skill a PhD does provide. When given even minor direction, they will generally take note.

I have known many young scholars in this cohort. I have mentored a number. Four elements have always contributed directly to their ongoing success.

1. Core identity formation. First, those of us who have a healthy connection with our PhD supervisor often do well as scholars. We grow in confidence that we do indeed belong to the guild of scholars and have had our abilities validated successfully. If the PhD supervisor is skilled at mentoring, there are probably other well-formed students who have built a network to which the young scholar can belong. I was fortunate to have a younger scholar, I. Howard Marshall of Aberdeen, Scotland, as my PhD supervisor/mentor. Howard eventually went on to become world-famous in New Testament studies, and countless students have now studied with him. Today Howard is a personal friend, and we have a remarkable community of "Marshall" graduates that meets annually at a national conference. We attend "Scottish" wine receptions as well, and all share the same stories about how we survived bravely living on Scotland's northeast coast. This anchored an identity for me and in some manner gave me a degree of security in who I was. Because I "belonged" to this community, I learned to travel to Tyndale Library in Cambridge, England (one of Europe's best theological libraries), where I met yet more American New Testament scholars studying in the UK. I was an "Aberdonian" and so I fit in. Today I like to return to Cambridge for my sabbaticals.

This same story could be told by an endless array of young scholars who live with the life-giving memory of some accolade, some interest, shown to them by a leading scholar. We are fragile at these moments, and we wonder if everyone is assessing us. I remember standing in the hallway at a national conference one year with a friend and the famous New Testament scholar James Dunn of Durham, England. My friend suddenly made a cynical remark about my PhD dissertation hoping to curry favor with Dunn at my expense. The trouble was my "friend" didn't realize that Dunn had been my external examiner at Durham, and he lit up quickly and rushed to my defense. "You're wrong, actually, it is a brilliant piece of work," is a sentence now decades old, but in memory, as fresh as if said yesterday.

This is what psychologists refer to as *core identity formation*, and if it isn't developed fully, young scholars will need to experience this formation early in their career from other influential sources such as a mentor or administrator. If this identity is never formed, uncertainty will stalk their adult lives and they will live with an unsatisfied quest for validation. They often will compensate with other unfortunate behaviors such as gathering cliques of students or employing negative attention-getting behavior (the "Pied Piper Professor" and the "campus radical"). The problem is a profound lack at the center of their soul, a question mark that has never been edited—the absence of a voice at a formative stage that told them that they mattered deeply. Well-disguised self-doubt will plague them unless something or someone intervenes early. I remember a scene in the wonderful film *The Help* (2011) where Aibileen Clark (played by Viola Davis) tells a neglected little girl in her care in Jackson, Mississippi: "You is kind, you is smart, you is important." These are words each of us needs to hear. Often.

I think of an endless list of young faculty I have known who would easily (though privately) refer to themselves as frauds. Impersonators. Interlopers in an academic world where they don't belong. And each of them is just waiting for that one moment when they will be unmasked. I know one talented junior faculty member who just cannot refer to himself as a "professor." *I'm a teacher at my college.* And I've heard one of his friends correct him. *You are a professor, not a teacher!* But what is at work here is not just nomenclature. These titles are hiding something else, some fear of presumption, some anxiety about being an impostor.

This is particularly true in colleges that are performance driven, perfectionist and constantly attuned to their reputation. Colleges that believe their students are "the best" will announce that they expect nothing less than "the best" faculty. And young faculty living within that culture will worry incessantly about their well-being and performance. For some, the stress this atmosphere produces is toxic and crippling. In one private college I know, the students built a Facebook page titled: "[college name]: Where your best is never good enough." It makes grim reading but unveils a cultural tendency that even students feel. Imagine faculty.

In such settings, without a firm sense of who we are, the anxiety of these toxic environments can be crippling. Still other young faculty cope with these anxieties by overcompensating—posturing, perhaps—to show others and themselves that they are indeed worthy of applause and just a bit brighter than everyone else. Such compensatory behavior only adds to the anxiety of the rest and creates communities that seem to exhaust rather than inspire.

2. Peer relationships. Second, peer relationships at an early stage either energize or cripple us. We enter our academic departments vulnerable, not knowing the verbal codes or understanding the subtle alliances that exist between professors. We need an interpreter, someone who will guide us through the minefields, explain how power is used, show us which secretaries are friendly, and give us tips to success. We need *safe* relationships with people outside the assessment system, people to whom we can admit our weaknesses and failings. These wholesome connections are necessary lifelines for proper development.

But some encounters of faculty with peers may be discouraging. Recently a new faculty member told me of an odd and disheartening experience. A midcareer professor came to her office during her first week and, rather than offering the usual niceties, pressed her: "So what did you publish this summer?" She had just finished her PhD, moved from abroad and had a baby all in the same summer. She was relieved when I understood and tried to give her an alternative perspective on this colleague and how vital it was for her to find other supportive relationships.

Such supportive peer relationships can form when casual gatherings take place away from senior faculty and administrators. I know one extroverted anthropologist who hosts parties at his house and "payday" gatherings at a local Irish pub. These are gathering places where young faculty can find assurance and affirmation. They need to tell the irreverent jokes that you cannot say on campus. "So how do I really get tenured?" is typical of the late-night chatter.

Wise institutions that are alert to formation will make these events happen for junior faculty. But they rarely work with administrative leadership. They must spring from a healthy faculty life itself.

These observations about the importance of peer affirmation have been confirmed by research data at Harvard's Graduate School of Education where college-specific research is done regularly. In 2013 Stanford University underwent an exhaustive study (with Harvard) and learned that faculty happiness is keyed (among other things) to a collegial environment where peers engage and express appreciation for their scholarship. Otherwise what results is "research isolation" in which the professor has no sense of connectedness to the larger purposes of the school. At Stanford, 40 percent of faculty said this described them. And many commented that in their culture everyone was "too busy" to notice or value them.[1]

Perhaps one antidote is to have a relationship with a mentor—and in the last ten years I have heard numerous young faculty tell me how much they wish they had one. This is a Cohort 2 or 3 professor who has an instinct for formative experiences, who is naturally affirming, who has retained an enthusiasm for teaching and believes strongly in the college. Weak departments will simply assign mentors on rotation without evaluating their skills or giving them direction. Thoughtful department leaders will outline the mentor's tasks, use only skilled faculty for the job, follow up with the mentor and guarantee that the mentoring relationship is confidential and not reported back to an assessment system. *Above all, it must be a safe relationship.* The unfortunate truth is that only a minority of midcareer and senior faculty will mentor well. Most will simply "check in" once in a while but find themselves preoccupied with their other professional tasks.

I have known young faculty who were "mentored" by senior faculty whom they never saw. In one case, no one had observed a young teacher's courses for two full years. Another young professor in the fine arts had been teaching for six months and wondered if his efforts were worthwhile. No one had visited his classes to validate his work. I asked casually over lunch if I could watch him some day teach a drawing class since I had never seen one. I just stood in the back and observed in amazement as he explained and modeled something called "negative space." He was good, really good. And it was easy to see how much the students liked him. I smiled after class and told him how genuinely talented he was. And later he remarked that just having someone older stand there and tell him how well he did was so renewing and confidence building.

---

[1]See the Stanford COACHE report from 2013 at the Harvard School of Graduate Education, http://isites.harvard.edu/icb/icb.do?keyword=coache&pageid=icb.page320671.

I don't know a thing about art. I didn't have to. I was just another adult—a generation older—giving him warm approval for what he was doing. About four months later he stopped me in the faculty dining room and told me again that he still had not been observed—and that my little visit and response meant everything to him.

Peer approval is crucial to us at every stage of our lives. Our peers are a mirror into which we look and decide what we are really like: from the ten-year-old boy who is told that his skateboarding skills are cool by the neighborhood gang, to the fifteen-year-old girl who is told her clothes are amazing by other girls whose opinions matter. Personal validation by peers contributes powerfully to whether we believe we are cool or amazing, smart or eloquent, or if we decide we are simply frauds because we've accepted our own worst self-criticism. Peers build those foundations that either inspire us to go on or cripple us.

The risk of publication rejection is directly related to this need for early peer approval. In peer-reviewed journals, young scholars can experience rejection or affirmation of their abilities. A young, gifted colleague recently received these comments from an anonymous peer reviewer, and this led to one of his earliest journal publications. I will edit it for brevity:

> This piece does an excellent job of relating to the objectives of [journal name].
>
> The article is well written. The thesis statement is clear and well argued. I would only suggest that a heading be inserted to designate the author's concluding statements.
>
> The article demonstrates a high level of academic facility. The author is well read and engaged with his primary authors of whom his paper is dealing with. The author may consider some more references to secondary work, but considering the limitations on length, it is not necessary in my estimation.
>
> Besides my very minor suggestions above, the paper is an

excellent piece of academic work and, in my opinion, should be published.

These comments were miraculous in their ability to transform and embolden. Once again, they were *validating*. In this case, the name of the scholar wasn't even known. The words were anonymous. But it did not matter. The writer was a peer scholar who had given him—his academic ability, his writing skills, his *core identity*—a thumbs up.

3. Student validation. The third element of Cohort 1 success is positive student experiences. I often ask my classes if they have any new teachers in their courses. They instinctively know if a professor is new, and they tell me that they sense the difference in confidence, classroom organization and mastery of the material. Then I surprise them: I say that *they* have more power than they realize to shape a young faculty member into a great professor. As students are they attentive? Respectful? On time? Do they give positive visual feedback? Do they express appreciation and interest in these teachers? Are they sitting anywhere near the front? I challenge them to take these professors to lunch on campus and get to know them personally. And it is a testimony to the sincerity of the students at Wheaton that they frequently take me up on it. They return glowing: *She was thrilled to go to the dining hall with us! He really notices when we are affirming and interested in the seminar. We really like her. I'm recommending him to all my friends.* A room full of disengaged students is toxic to the young professor; a room full of enthusiastic students is a gift beyond measure.

Young faculty have antennae alert to rejection and failure among students. Since class registration now takes place online, I have seen young faculty check online hourly just to see if their classes fill up quickly. They compare their sections to other sections as the registration tally changes. It must be like watching a horse race. The scorecard is the tally of student interest, and the winner is the person who has a full waiting list, not empty seats.

The great temptation is to see *popularity* with students as the sign of success. Of course the trauma of rejection and acceptance has likely been with us since we first entered school at five or six. And even if those in authority don't set the ground rules, we are quite happy to make them for ourselves. So we are easily convinced, asking ourselves: *Is not enrollment one sign of success?* But it isn't entirely our fault. Administrative leaders often affirm this view with the public comment that honors some but shames others. I have heard each of these: "This is Professor X whose classes are always in high demand." "This is Professor X—the genius of the faculty." "He is one of our student favorites." "I wish everyone could teach like she does." "This professor is one of our treasures." After hearing one of those public accolades, we wonder: *What if no one ever says something like that about me?*

The chief problem with the pursuit of student popularity is that it robs us of our integrity in the classroom. I remember years when I was so preoccupied with how students were responding to me that I feared saying or doing things that might make them dislike me. There were times when students misbehaved—but I remained silent. Times when a class needed to hear something painful or discomforting and I failed to risk their rejection. In a word, the quest for popularity robs us of a prophetic voice. One of the great gifts of aging is that you can begin to realize that popularity is fleeting, while integrity and honesty are more important. It is absolutely renewing to suddenly be set free from the race to be popular.

This is the reason I urge young faculty to never (never, ever) look at the website Rate My Professor. This is a well-known site where students can record anonymous comments about faculty at virtually every college in America. The problem is that the students who do this often have a reason to do it: they frequently are unhappy or they are your fans. This means that the great satisfied middle of your class just won't log on. Your fans and your detractors will make an appearance. Those of us who have experience with carefully quantified student evaluative instruments know how useless this site really is. Besides, does anyone really want to be rated as "hot"?

These ratings can also be manipulated by groups of students who together either inflate a professor's profile or bring him/her down. One young professor I knew discovered that four students had utterly criticized him unfairly, and he was devastated. Some of his faculty friends had a solution: they each logged on anonymously as if they were students and inflated his score with made-up compliments. Today *Rate My Professor* has a tab for faculty to give their own feedback to these comments. It is hard to imagine a more foolish move.

To avoid the risk of losing popularity, young faculty often make two common errors. They either become overly familiar with students or they become too distant and harsh (thereby insulating themselves from the race). The first error is understandable and springs from the mistaken notion that if "I am just one of them, I'll be liked." Any parent who has had teenagers knows the catastrophe guaranteed by this plan. Popularity isn't won through wearing Abercrombie or knowing the latest about Taylor Swift or Ariana Grande or Coldplay. Or pretending to be a fan of John Legend. Students privately refer to these profs as "posers."

The second error is equally tragic. To shore up authority and confidence, some young scholars become authoritarian and distant. "I really don't care what they think" is the mantra. But deep down the very opposite is the truth. This is simply compensatory behavior, shielding us from the pain of what we fear might happen. Some of us become weirdly eccentric or strangely esoteric, thinking that this is the "role" that students are expecting to find. Besides, it is a role that frees us from having anything to do with popular culture. "*American Idol*? Is that something religious? Last night I was busy reading Chaucer." Seriously. The skilled academic is warm, approachable and fully in charge of the classroom. He or she does not need the social reinforcement of being "popular."

College students are not looking for a new friend; they are looking for friendly adults who will remain adults.

Eager, receptive students make an eager, responsive professor. Cynical, negative students will make a despairing, self-critical professor. In the first two semesters, an intuitive mentor will listen carefully to how the young teacher is feeling in classes and frequently attend just to give feedback. This is one of the most potent and long-lasting formative contributions we can make to a young professor's life.

I recall mentoring a new colleague who had a particularly difficult section. Something clearly was going wrong. So I agreed to stop in, sit quietly in the back and observe. It was horrible. Students were talking audibly to each other, texting on their phones, and then it happened: a young woman (who thought she was funny) stood up during class and announced loudly, "I've had it with this boring class, 'Dr. Smith.' I'm outta here." She dramatically grabbed her backpack and marched out slamming the door loudly. For the first time in years, I was dumbstruck. As was the professor. He didn't know what to do, and because I was there he was doubly embarrassed. Silence hung over the room like a pall.

So I stood up quietly, looked at the students who were stone silent, and asked them how any young woman thought she had license for that sort of disrespect. My tone probably conveyed more than my words. I felt like I was giving a firm late-Friday-night lecture to a recalcitrant teenager. I went on: "Dr. Smith is a brilliant scholar. You're lucky to have him. Personally I think your friend who just exited owes him an apology. Please convey this to her." Those forty students knew I meant business. And one later told me how good it felt that someone had spoken up "for law and order." The apology was delivered to "Dr. Smith" within twenty-four hours.

Some immature, intellectually gifted students sense weakness in young faculty and exploit it. Female faculty tell me that this is an acute problem particularly for them. At every one of the three colleges where I've worked, female professors have described the most remarkable challenges to their authority: from comments about their wardrobe, to their figures (yes, their figures or their weight), to their competence. One heard this in class: "That's what you say, but Dr. Jones [a man] disagrees with you." The silence that hangs afterward is as threatening as it can be.

I remember once being challenged repeatedly by the grandson of one of our well-known retired college trustees. He was immature, a freshman, and it was awful. His final gambit after one of his provocative questions: "If this is what you believe, Dr. Burge, maybe we should report you to the president." I escorted him into the hallway, closed the door very calmly, and we had a clarifying conversation. Three days before his graduation, he came to me and apologized for events then four years old. Before he left the college, he wanted to clean up the past and be released from the shame of those immature moments. Today I count him as a friend.

Until the young faculty member gains instinctive gracious control over a room filled with forty precocious nineteen-year-olds, they are vulnerable to harm.

4. College validation. The final and fourth area contributing to the health of Cohort 1 comes from the college itself. Virtually everyone the young professor meets stands in a power relationship with him or her, and they sense it. Chairs, deans and provosts have astounding power to encourage or harm. So do senior faculty. Indifference ("What was your name again?") or insensitivity ("How is that publication you promised coming along?") will always have potent effects. I remember returning to the college after life-changing international experiences eager to tell *anyone* about them. A college leader saw me on the first day back and repeated what I learned was to be a common refrain: "So how was Egypt? I'll have to hear about it sometime." That time never came, again and again and again. Simply: he wanted to care, but he was always too busy to *really care* about most of us.

Sadly, a few of our leaders are either unskilled in interpersonal relationships (either bruising or neglecting faculty) or find themselves too busy to contribute thoughtfully to what a person needs. The quest for efficiency and productivity is often the plague that subverts us when we know we should be spending thoughtful time with younger teachers but do not.

Many years ago I lived through a really tough patch in my own personal life. Few people knew about it, but it was debilitating and I feared it was soon going to affect my work. And I made a mistake. Since I was in a Christian college, I assumed that an important administrator would be empathic, supportive and wise in his counsel. Instead, after I told him what was going on, he told me some very strange story about how military sergeants don't really want to know about how the troops feel—they just want to make sure they can fight the war. He then rocked back in his chair with hands folded behind his head and stared at me. It was one of those moments you don't forget.

On the other hand, I recall a remarkable administrator I knew in the 1990s. A major part of his job was faculty development. So each week he intentionally walked around campus, strolled through departments, and when a door was open, he'd stop in just to casually visit. He was like a faculty chaplain who knew how to strengthen faculty through encouragement. But he also could discipline and guide with a confident hand. When he asked, "How are you?" you knew he meant it and he had the time to listen—genuinely listen. When administrators have these relational skills, we treasure them. One new administrator once told me: "I need to remain distant in order to keep my authority." I thought it was a sad perspective on life.

My first few years of teaching witnessed some of the strangest administrative attempts to validate faculty one could imagine. The college delegated to the senior class a vote to determine the "best" list for the faculty. "Best teacher," "best personality" and "best dresser" were just a few of the more memorable categories. Fortunately they missed "most likely to succeed." It was a beauty contest built in the worst imaginable form.

Now shift to a change Wheaton made about twelve years ago. Rather than have a "best teacher" award at the end of the year, the college's provost designed "faculty achievement awards"—many of them to be distributed each spring. Each year a number of faculty are singled out and given a plaque, a load reduction for one year and a tidy sum of cash. Once you've won, you are ineligible for seven years. It has been brilliant. And it has done a great deal to build up faculty who doubted their own successes.

The skills I grew to value in parenting are the very skills that hallmark the effective leader whose task is the formation and development of young faculty. It is love wed to discipline, or perhaps genuine interest and affection combined with firm guidance. When the balance is discovered, good things result. When it is not, compensatory coaching from peers and mentors is necessary to interpret the situation and figure out how to thrive.

CLASSIC RISKS IN COHORT 1

Not every young faculty member succeeds. The goal of his or her efforts is to fit into this new career, to win the respect of peers and the confidence of the administration. But there are predictable pitfalls; some of them are unique to this cohort, and sometimes they end a career.

1. Skills failure. The most obvious problem comes with what I term a skills failure. Every new teacher fails, but in this case, it seems that fundamental abilities as a teacher or a scholar are not in place. I recall working closely with an international teacher who was just beginning his career. We thought he would bring remarkable diversity to the classroom. And yet his cultural distance from our students was unbridgeable. As a first-generation Asian scholar, he expected the students to be immediately respectful and quiet. He read notes to them from behind the lectern in a quiet voice and never looked up. I urged him to make some basic changes to adapt to our cultural setting, but he could not.

Within a few weeks the students began acting out. They could not understand this performance they were watching and did not like it. He stayed in his office alone with the door shut as he wrote endless scholarly articles. In a word, he made no emotional connections with the students, didn't find it necessary, and in our highly relational campus culture, his reputation eroded rapidly. He was failing as a teacher.

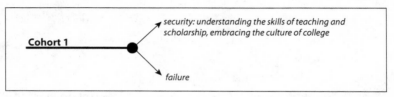

Figure 1.2. Cohort 1—two paths

I believe that good teaching can be learned, but for early success it requires some fundamental skills that are evidenced at the beginning. Things such as verbal communication, personal transparency, agile thinking, a sense of humor, healthy self-criticism, native intellectual aptitude, confidence and curiosity are each components of the successful teacher. Every teacher will have different combinations of these, but rarely will a teacher succeed without some of each. And where entire categories are missing—such as verbal communication skills—failure may result.

One new faculty member I knew once was so apprehensive when he stood before a class that he registered overt defensiveness every time a student asked a question. They couldn't understand it. One of his students told me: "We couldn't tell if it was arrogance or fear, but he just couldn't or wouldn't answer any innocent questions." Finally five weeks into the semester, he announced that no questions would be entertained in class any longer and that all questions had to be submitted by email. The young professor was trying to build a protective barrier to keep from being challenged or questioned in areas where he felt weak. And as the semester progressed, his relationship with the class rapidly crumbled. At moments like this one would hope that a good mentor would have spotted the problem, stepped in with advice and helped avoid the disaster.

Many younger faculty members have benefited from watching films that have a prominent motif of strong teachers who in some manner captivate their students' interests with remarkable skills. Faculty have recommended a number of titles, but these are repeated again and again: *The Paper Chase, The Emperor's Club, Dead Poets' Society, Dangerous Minds, Freedom Writers, Stand and Deliver, Mr. Holland's Opus, Waiting for Superman, The Prime of Ms. Jean Brodie.*

The other expected skill is scholarship. And yet there are some who experience an odd sort of paralysis when putting words on a page. Scholarly writing is a part of the academic trade, and without it, some will wonder if the young faculty member has joined the great conversations within the discipline. Not every scholar is a writer. But every scholar needs to be contributing at some level to their guild either by reading papers, organizing meetings, offering fine arts performances or writing reviews. The dilemma comes when a person fails to join those "great conversations" in any meaningful way. After their PhD they withdraw from their disciplinary peers and hope that by teaching successfully the college will waive their lack of scholarship. It rarely works.

2. Assimilation failure. The second risk in this cohort is the inability of the young professor to embrace the institutional mission or culture of the college. This means that at some profound level, he or she cannot champion what the college stands for. The person seems out of step with the values that are promoted. If it is a Christian College, she may disagree with its commitments or theological perspectives. He may become cynical early on regarding the school's leaders or its history. Every college or university requires some level of conformity to its academic and social culture. Some schools require strict loyalty; others are widely diverse and invite divergence. But for a teacher to neglect this or to intentionally repudiate it is to invite disaster.

I remember teaching once at a moderately liberal Christian college. Doctrinal conformity was rarely discussed. Faculty debated if the school should even affiliate with its parent denomination (which supplied considerable funding). As a young scholar, I had to learn to fit in even though in some respects I was more conservative. However, I had another friend for whom this entire culture was grating. "The college has lost its mooring." "This ought to be a state school." "The denomination should just cut it loose." These were common refrains from him, and sometimes he was right. But he had to make up his mind: Was he willing to fit in or not?

Since my family background was Lutheran, it was a culture shock when I joined Wheaton's faculty in the 1990s. I didn't realize that I had entered the evangelical subculture. There was a vocabulary people didn't know they were using. There was humor that seemed out of bounds. In my first year, I noted in class that I believed that women could indeed be ordained to the ministry. That same week a student from that class was having lunch with me and asked, "Dr. Burge, do you think you are *really* an evangelical?" The query stemmed entirely from our discussion on gender. In those days, it was assumed that evangelicalism had reached a consensus on women's ordination. They should (it was assumed) stay out of the pulpit. Or as one senior faculty member once told me, "Gary, I've never met a *real* New Testament scholar who believed in the ordination of women."

This does not mean we have to conform entirely to the campus culture. Differences enrich our campus life. But we do have to discern the degree to which that culture is *conforming*. Some campuses celebrate diversity and see it as a strength; others look for greater homogeneity. Some colleges define themselves by how they guard the perimeters of what is right and what is wrong. They can create a defensive atmosphere where faculty worry if they fit in. Others work from the convictions held at the center and worry less about marginal issues. They are more open, and it may feel like anyone can fit in. Some refer to the first type of college culture as "confessionally bounded"—always aware of the boundaries. The second type of college is "confessionally centered"—eager to promote what is believed without defensiveness.

Without discernment, the new faculty member can find him/herself at odds with the community. I remember a fine new scholar who joined our college one year. He was self-described as a "liberal Democrat from Oregon" and he enjoyed playing up that identity. But what happened when his new college world liked to wed Republican politics with evangelical piety? The conflicts both with students and faculty were inevitable. Today he is flourishing in a school that fits him perfectly.

I've often wondered how these sorts of atmospheres evolve. No one dictates these patterns from the president's office. Nothing is in writing. In some cases, very liberal and very conservative religious schools will look for theological and spiritual *consistency* in order to remain faithful to their legacy. And therefore such schools will struggle with building diversity within their faculty. At some colleges, minority faculty will confide that they just don't feel like they fit. They say that there isn't room for their vocabulary, interests or commitments. One director of multicultural affairs tells me that he has to coach minorities in how to survive in the "crosscultural" world of their new and culturally foreign college.

Simply put, colleges have cultures—even though they don't realize it—and reading those cultural clues correctly is vital to success.

3. Peer groups. Throughout our lives we are shaped by the friends we keep. Parents worry about "those kids" that might host the wrong parties, experiment with adult entertainments or exhibit unhelpful attitudes. They steer their own kids toward the "good influences" who will bring wholesome attitudes. Why should adulthood be any different?

The issue is that we unconsciously mimic the colleagues we work with. Ron Friedman at the University of Rochester has studied how mimicking behavior is both habitual and unconscious throughout our lives. But the workplace is where it shows up starkly. He writes,

The people we work with shape our thoughts, influence our creative thinking, and ultimately determine the quality of our work. By choosing to spend the majority of our waking hours with a particular set of people, we are not only determining the tenor of our daily experiences, we are defining the person we will eventually become. . . .

If research on motivational synchronicity has revealed anything it is this: Our colleagues influence us in more ways than we recognize.[2]

I recall joining the faculty of one college and feeling eager to find a peer group that would decode my new world and give me a cohort to identify with. It wasn't long before I located a circle of about twelve faculty that met for coffee in one professor's office while everyone else was at chapel. The timing alone was ironic. I attended weekly for about two or three months and soon began to feel some unease about the entire gathering. These were faculty with five to fifteen years experience, and they were deeply cynical about most matters that came up for discussion: the president, the provost, most deans, the trustees, faculty load, religious identity, creedal commitments—did I mention the president? All of it was very clever and wickedly funny. And you had to be "on board" to be a part of the circle. The temptation to join up was enormous. Now that I think back on this, it reminds me of a sort of delayed adolescence worked out in later life. We were powerful because we could tell stories. And occasionally some of them were true.

I have to admit that it was fun. I thought I'd discovered the in crowd where snarky comments and knowing gestures reigned. The catch was this: I realized that my attitudes toward the college and its leaders were being shaped by these people. I liked every one of them individually, but when they slipped into that conspiratorial hour, new personas emerged. I don't know why, but one week I simply decided never to return. I re-

---

[2]R. Friedman, "Motivation Is Contagious," *Psychology Today,* March/April 2013, p. 50.

member walking intentionally to chapel that Wednesday and knowing I'd made at least one unusual virtuous decision for that semester.

Some younger faculty never make the right choice. They think they've found the shamans who will tell all—who will bring them under wing, who will whisper the secrets of success and interpret who leverages power. But what settles into their minds is an ambiguous sense of commitment to the mission of the college. Enthusiasm for your school is subtly diluted into something cautious, something jaded, perhaps something suspicious. I have known wonderful faculty who have landed in this place. And tragically, after a long enough time, they don't know how to extricate themselves *because they no longer see what's wrong with it.* They've completely taken in the values of the group. And their only hope is almost to depart for a new place of employment.

A senior faculty member once told me this: Look for who is respected and admired by peers and students and *intentionally* plan personal time with them. Make a lunch date. Stop by their office. Ask for their help. Even good Christian colleges have healthy and unhealthy people. Oddly, the unhealthy ones generate a kind of intoxicating power. And if it isn't recognized, the same intoxication will become a part of the new professor.

4. Toxic anxiety. Occasionally we can experience a complete collapse of confidence. This is rare, but I have seen it enough times—and watched young faculty suffer under its weight—that I now realize it is more common than we think. It is akin to living with chronic depression. You simply cannot tell anyone you're depressed *again* today. You have to behave as if you are chipper and enthusiastic. And it takes enormous mental and emotional energy to support your happy facade.

Creativity begins to vanish daily; spontaneity disappeared long ago; genuine humor is a friend from a distant memory. Your energy seems to slip away daily and you're waiting to be found out. Every day gets worse—it is a cycle—and if by November your confidence has eroded, by April the natural consequences of this self-doubt convince you that indeed you are in the wrong job. You *cannot hear* the encouraging words of the friends who instinctively want to pump you up.

The truth is this: such anxiety is not just similar to depression; such anxiety actually can lead to depression, and when left undiagnosed or not remedied, it may become a habit of living and thinking. It is vital to know that such ongoing anxiety or depression can actually change us and become a habit that seems almost impossible to end. But there is good news: it can be remedied with therapeutic and/or medical interventions.

I have observed this despair in two ways: faculty who have convinced themselves that they cannot teach (because students do not like them) or that they cannot write (because they are not true scholars). In some cases they are convinced that their peers have decided to disregard them (because their views are no longer worthy of consideration). Their self-talk becomes increasingly destructive. Their demeanor gradually changes. And eventually their best friends sense that something is wrong but they don't know what. Occasionally a casual word slips—few hear it—but the young professor is having a harder and harder time concealing the toxicity living just beneath the surface.

Help must be immediate and swift. It is the equivalent of throwing a lifeline to a drowning victim and smacking them with the rope just so they'll see it and grab hold. It must jar them, because they no longer believe they can be saved and have conceded that all is lost. A trusted friend or mentor with good instincts will spot this and speak to what is going on relentlessly. Not once, but again and again. They will probe how severe it is and recommend interventions. If left alone, the faculty member will descend into places no one wants to go, and the great promise of their work will begin to evaporate.

Let me reiterate that this is rare. But if it happens, young faculty will suffer in silence—and such isolation is precisely the setting that guarantees professional doom. They need to hear at high volume:

Anyone who has come this far is a person of high promise. Any other voice is false and will only sabotage you. We need someone to tell us to stop listening to those voices and to listen instead to those who know us well and can affirm us.

5. Friendship and resilience. There is growing evidence that one of the most important predictors of well-being and resilience in life has less to do with competence and everything to do with community. That is, the ability to make genuine friendships, not professional associations, is one of the most important keys to perseverance and health. My own observation is that these connections, which are formed when we are young scholars, are the ones we will value for the duration of our careers. We have a capacity in our thirties (an interest? a willingness to be vulnerable? a youthful transparency?) that mysteriously dissipates as we age unless we put it to use intentionally when we are younger. But if we do not pursue these relationships with intention, isolation can result; before we know it, we are the solitary scholar who in midlife has numerous "conference friendships" but few profound relationships with people to whom we can disclose our deepest struggles or our most vital needs for encouragement.

Many have also noted a gender variable here. My casual observation has been that women frequently create these relationships more readily than men. I know young female faculty who are "writing partners," which means that they simply get together weekly to write at the same desk, keep each other going and chat now and then. I know other young faculty women who are in small groups, meeting in evenings. For years there was a women's "lunch table" at our college that met once each week. As someone once said, women are the social glue that holds society together. Perhaps they were right.

Once this gender variable is noticed, its evidence shows up everywhere. In my own neighborhood, women are out "walking" regularly. Or perhaps I should say "talking while they walk." It is common to see three women shoulder to shoulder at 7:30 a.m. exercising through our neighborhood. Curiously, I have yet to see a single example of two or three men doing the same. They may run together, but it is a solitary affair. A male colleague told me: "When I get home from playing golf, my wife always asks, 'So how are Peter's wife and kids?' I have to say I don't know. 'So what did you talk about for three hours in that golf cart?' My answer: the score, his last shot—I think he mentioned something about his job. I know it's lame, but we just don't chat." I've shared this story with a few of my male friends and they all laugh and "get it" immediately.

I explored this with a colleague who is a psychologist, and he led me to a whole world of literature that is examining the emotional inhibitions of men in our culture and how they are socialized as children to be alone, competitive and emotionally inaccessible. Mary Pipher popularized these studies originally with her well-known *Reviving Ophelia: Saving the Selves of Adolescent Girls* (1994). Not long after, Harvard's William Pollack decided to follow this with a study of his own: *Real Boys: Rescuing Our Sons from the Myths of Boyhood* (1998). It made for sobering reading. I began to see remarkable things about my own childhood, how I've been socialized, and how the community of men around me relate to one another. Pollack's analysis is devastating. He talks at length about how young boys are "hardened" as a protective reflex against shame, and the only permissible emotion that they are encouraged to activate quickly is anger in all its refined forms. Studies of storytelling to young male and female children in our culture illustrate this quickly: girls are given narratives of emotional drama or nurturing; boys are supplied with narratives about heroic retaliation, combat or conflict. It all goes a long way to understanding how highly educated adult men build sophisticated worlds that are nevertheless combative, competitive and isolated (even though they would barely dare to admit it). In the academy we don't do this with swords, we do it with resumes.

I mention this now because it is a vital risk for each of us. One of the important findings of Pollack is that young boys deeply desire intimacy just as much as girls. But they are either denied it or express it with one another in ways that go unrecognized. However, this risk of isolation is a danger that can be addressed more easily when we are young than when we are older. But if we don't address it, when we enter the final chapters of our career in Cohort 3, it can become a severe crisis with devastating implications. The alternative is something I've seen dozens of times: the brilliant, solitary, verbally barbed, well-published, competitive scholar who has no friends. And by fifty-five he doesn't know how to make a true friend.

Our resiliency will be closely tied to the emotional transparency and trust we share with the community we live in. But of course, if we are busy all the time and competitive with those relationships, such gifts of community will rarely find us.

6. *Unique issues for women.* Women who read an early version of this manuscript identified the same issue: that there are unique challenges that pertain to them as faculty and not to their male peers. Three issues are prominent, but each is not relevant to every woman.

First, in some collegiate settings young female faculty are quickly sexualized in the imaginations of their male students. Students may take astonishing liberties with comments about their professors' weight, clothes, hair, even their figures. I have heard these stories so many times over the years that my skepticism about it has been completely defeated. Young female faculty are treated differently, and for some, this is a deeply discouraging and demeaning experience. The support of senior women faculty and male colleagues is essential. And when it is reported, it must be believed.

Second, women will report that in some cases students will consider them weak or insufficiently skilled or easily challenged. And soon they find themselves fielding comments in class that I've never once heard in my career. They may be challenged to see if their knowledge is sufficient. They may be contrasted publicly with male faculty. They may be asked to tell their academic pedigree. Students may drop their class and report to their friends a lack in confidence in having a woman teacher. In conservative Christian circles there are even students who dislike having a female instructor based on theological grounds.

Third, women will describe the difficulty of negotiating career and family commitments. If a PhD is earned by, say, thirty, then it is no surprise that married women on the faculty will want to start a family within the next few years if they have not done so already. Will there be institutional support for this decision—something in our culture men barely need to consider? Will there be understanding if a class is missed because a child is sick? Does the college provide generous maternity leave? Has the college considered offering childcare on campus so female faculty can connect more closely with their children as is done in the corporate world? In its own self-analysis of faculty progress in this area in 2009, Auburn University decided to make this a priority and faculty noticed (particularly female faculty), making Auburn's programs stand out from its peers. Having children, raising children and finding creative ways to balance family and professional commitments is a hallmark of teaching at Auburn.[3]

Women have told me that they know immediately who understands their plight and who does not. Oddly, they report that it is sometimes older, senior women who "toughed it out" early in their careers who are the least supportive. Perhaps this is a generational issue, and as women increasingly enter the professional workforce, younger leaders will be ready to accommodate them.

7. Personal boundaries. This is a small (and rare) issue, but its consequences are so devastating that it begs attention. Young faculty are not far in age from the very students they teach. We may be twenty-nine (as I was my first year) and our students may be twenty-one. And if we see graduate students, the margin is smaller.

The problem is this: we may have natural inclinations to socialize with (even date) students we teach. Young students looking for role

---

[3]See the Auburn COACHE report from 2009 at the Harvard School of Graduate Education, http://isites.harvard.edu/icb/icb.do?keyword=coache&pageid=icb.page320671.

models may be enamored of us; some may be looking for parent figures; others are simply attracted to who we are: (apparently) smart, (apparently) confident, obviously employed, established, older. Imagine a young faculty member who may not have an easy life at home or no validation from their college—now surrounded by fawning twenty-year-olds. The trap is as inevitable as it is lethal.

I note this only because I have seen two faculty members completely ruin their careers thanks to such relationships. I've seen others come close. I remember sitting one day in a young colleague's office when in walked an attractive senior woman in a very alluring outfit. He lapsed into flirtatious banter with her about the advantages of wearing short skirts to class. She was enjoying it. So was he. I think his wife would have been less amused.

Wise colleges generally have firm guidelines about student/faculty interpersonal boundaries. Denying or bending them (with nice rationalizations) is guaranteed to result in disaster.

But oddly, this issue can turn in an entirely different direction. For younger faculty, particularly single faculty, relationships among colleagues of the opposite sex can be rewarding, sometimes romantic and in many cases lead to marriage. This is all good in my estimation. But there are other more complex relationships that can evolve, particularly between people married to other people—or single faculty who begin to be emotionally involved with married faculty. We work closely together, and it is inevitable that close relationships result. The human heart has an enormous capacity for self-deception. It is a courageous act of love for friends to tell friends not to go off a cliff that they cannot see. I've seen this happen twice. And it always ends poorly.

THE CLOSING OF COHORT 1

Life in Cohort 1 (as with all the cohorts) has a beginning and an end. It begins with your first contract. And it ends (hopefully) with security. In some cases this comes in the form of tenure. In other cases, it is a multiyear contract (depending on the college). But essentially it is a growing sense that you are safe; the institution has decided that you should remain, and as a professor your contribution is valued. I think the reigning word is *security*—one of the principal things younger faculty yearn to possess. Therefore a turning point comes here, a crossroads even. Cohort 1 ends when a threshold is passed, and every professor knows it.

Colleges will commonly publish lists of "promotable strengths" or "tenure criteria." Some of these tell the truth and some do not. For example, some will list "scholarship" alongside "committee service" as if they were of equal weight. I have never seen someone denied tenure for being disengaged with the faculty or failing to show up for committees. But I have seen faculty tenured who were successfully published but rarely attended faculty meetings or rarely accepted a committee assignment. What is going on here?

The reality is this: colleges have criteria that are ranked—some count for more than others, and as college leadership evolves, these rankings will shift as well. (At my own college they have shifted measurably just during my last fifteen years.) Colleges also have criteria that are not explicit (though this is rarely admitted). Discerning how this works is crucial. There are four criteria that every college will seek, and if these are mastered, security is all but assured. A good mentor will know how to discern these and give needed guidance.

1. Teaching. This is the heart of a college's effort since it lies near the center of its mission and directly affects those who support it: the students. Every good college will have a thoughtful teaching assessment program that the young faculty member must know thoroughly.

2. Scholarship. This means that in some manner, you are engaged in the larger conversations outside the classroom. You are digesting new ideas; you are organizing new paths forward; you are making a contribution. Here too colleges will have a program for assessing this feature of our careers, and many of them will take publication lists seriously. I have found that administrators are often conflicted when explaining how this is done. "We are not counting articles" is often stated, but the reality is that they may be doing just that.

These are the two chief criteria, and they will constantly surface in written evaluations of our work. They are also easily assessed since objective criteria (the resume, student evaluations) can be employed. However, there are other less objective criteria that also operate, and even though they are subjective, they can influence the outcome of your career.

3. *Embracing the culture.* I referred earlier to the problem of "assimilation failure" in which a faculty member fails to understand or accept the social reality that the college creates. And since a Christian college will have a decidedly religious ethos that weighs heavily on its culture, understanding, accepting and living within this religious world is vital. The more intentionally this value is practiced, the more seriously it will be taken.

4. *Corporate life.* This refers to full participation in the life of the community, volunteering for student activities, joining committees, championing things that matter to the campus culture. I've spoken in dorms, helped student clubs sponsor films, served on student panels, contributed to the student newspaper and joined numerous faculty committees. All of this says: "I'm on board."

The important thing about these last two criteria is that they cannot be measured. They are intuited. And when the college leadership intuits that you may not "fit," they will begin looking more carefully, perhaps less charitably, at the objective criteria on which they base their decisions.

Some examples may help. Imagine an outspoken evangelical professor who is openly critical of how the college where he or she works has "abandoned its legacy." This may be true, but it won't help win tenure. Or imagine a successful professor who decides to become Roman Catholic in a college that is decidedly conservative Protestant. Even if he signs the statement of faith, still, the leadership may believe something is wrong, and he will be in jeopardy. I referred earlier to the "liberal Democrat from Oregon" who was a fine teacher and scholar. He was surprised when his contract wasn't renewed but didn't realize that some people of influence didn't like how he pushed the culture. Truth is, he was just different. He had to find a different college with a better cultural fit. He did. And today he is happy and successful.

Simply put: if we are happy and flourishing, if we enjoy what we do with students, if we continue to be stimulated by our disciplinary interests, if we respect the campus culture—religious, social, political—moving to "security" is not something that should worry us. Young faculty often ask me if I think they will be tenured as if it will be decided one afternoon. Tenure is being decided year by year in the accumulation of annual assessments that are gathering in the professor's file. The outcome of a tenure decision is rarely a surprise. And when it is, there has been some failure by the professor to understand *who they are* in the college or there has been some failure by the college to give formative input along the way.

Addendum

The Mentor's Role

When a department assigns a faculty member to mentor an incoming younger colleague, it is a critical decision that will form the outlook for the junior professor for years. Some senior faculty will take an interest in mentoring; many will not. Simply assigning faculty on a rotation to mentor incoming new hires is a mistake. Caroline Simon's helpful book *Mentoring for Mission* (2004) provides concrete ideas for how a mentoring relationship can become one of the most formative experiences in a professor's career. She notes how one motive for pursuing this is compassion for how difficult it is to join a new college and faculty. She writes:

> One important motive for mentoring is compassion rooted in remembering the apprehensions and confusions you yourself may have had in taking on your first full-time teaching job. Empathy

can move veteran faculty to make time in their busy schedules to help junior faculty find their way in a new environment.[4]

As faculty begin to reflect on what that role might look like, the following elements should be a baseline for what might transpire. But you may be a junior faculty member, with a mentor, and you'd like more input from him/her. Go over this list together; perhaps you can read Simon's book. Either way, ask for the sort of formative help you need.

1. *Making friends.* This is so fundamental, it barely needs to be said. New faculty are looking for a few friends whom they can trust. Some new faculty will welcome overtures of friendship; others will be more cautious. Nevertheless, the offer of friendship is essential as a beginning.

Things to do:

- At the close of the first day of classes, check in with them, asking how things went on their first day. See if they have any needs you can meet. Have they made friends with the photocopier yet? Sometimes it is as simple as just knowing their teaching schedule.

- During the first week of classes, schedule a lunch date in which you go together to the faculty dining room or "the restaurant" where faculty gather. When I taught at North Park University in Chicago there was no faculty dining room—but there was a small Swedish restaurant just across the street that served the same function.

- During the first month of the semester, have them over to your home for a meal. Better still, include some of your other colleagues so that new friendships are made.

- Don't hesitate to arrange more personal conversation times throughout the semester.

2. *Getting assimilated.* Every college has its code language ("So is Parks Hall for women only?" "What is 'the Beamer' anyway?"), its

---

[4]Caroline J. Simon, *Mentoring for Mission: Nurturing New Faculty at Church-Related Colleges* (Grand Rapids: Eerdmans, 2003), p. 13.

secrets for how things are done ("So whom do I call in the IT department?") and minefields that should be avoided ("What? I can't make color copies as handouts?"). There are helpful secretaries and those who are less helpful. Even finding the buildings can be daunting.

Things to do:

- During the first week of class—or perhaps on the first day of class—walk to chapel or an assembly with them so that they see how it's done. If there is no chapel, join them for any other important convocation.

- Make a note of the first faculty meeting in your calendar and offer to go there together. Entering your first faculty meeting is filled with social risks. Where do you sit? Where are the refreshments? Who will talk to me? One small group of faculty I know missed an entire semester of faculty meetings because they didn't know about them!

- When you get special mailings (such as the student registration schedule) or have to decipher the cryptic final exam schedule, anticipate how these might look to someone new.

- Does the college have an opening banquet? Suggest that you go along together with your spouses.

3. The classroom. The classroom is the main venue where work is done. And the junior professor needs to start off confidently.

Things to do:

- Before the semester begins, suggest that together you check out the classroom that is assigned. This is especially crucial if digital technology is going to be used. Make sure they have keys to any security cabinets and any needed passwords, and that they know how to run the screen, computers and sound. Give it a test run.

- The registrar will distribute a class roster (or it will be online). Be sure they know how to find it, read it and use it at the first class.

- Provide suggestions for what to do on that ominous first day. It is easy to forget what that felt like. Social risks abound, and for some students, this will create their first impression of the teacher that will remain for weeks. The online journal *The Teaching Professor* has a valuable issue devoted to just this topic.[5]

- Attend two different classes within the first four weeks of the term and take notes. If your department has one, complete a class observation form. This is a friendly visit, not reported back to the department chair, and if significant trust is present, it can be a constructive, helpful source of feedback.

- Encourage the use of a written, midsemester student evaluation that is used only by the professor and not shared with the department. This instrument is for self-awareness, not departmental assessment. I developed a very simple one-page document that does the trick. In narrative form, ask students: (1) What is working well in this class for you? (2) What is not working so well in this class for you? Then at the bottom of the page I provide a small scale from one to ten and ask, (3) On a scale of 1–10, mark if this is the most helpful class you've had (10) or one of the least helpful (1).

---

[5]"The First Day of Class: Advice and Ideas," *The Teaching Professor*, 1989, 3(7), 1-2.

WILL I FIND SUCCESS?

Elation. This was my initial feeling after I was tenured for the first time. The phone call from the dean. The quiet applause at the faculty meeting. The congratulatory handshake. The brief article in the student paper. It seemed as if I was living in a different relationship to everything around me: the faculty, the college, students, even the campus landscaping. I had passed some test, won some medal; I could now stand sure-footed in a way I had not before. It is paralleled by the moment when a PhD committee awards you your degree. Something has been given that will not be taken away.

But it is also an odd mix of feelings. One new Cohort 2 professor told me that her pursuit of career security (and tenure) was so intense and her work for it so hard, when it finally came she felt empty. "Is this all there is?" Without some concrete goal in front of her any longer, without the adrenaline-producing tension of summative evaluations, motivation felt like it was slipping away.

This sort of malaise is typical of those of us who reach midcareer, find security and wonder what is left. This phenomenon is well-documented (and is not to be confused with a midlife crisis) but perhaps best described in a fascinating article by Jonathan Rauch in a recent issue of *The Atlantic*. Rauch describes his own trajectory thus:

At age forty-seven he finally found security in academia by gaining tenure. But while he felt satisfied, he felt trapped. He was financially secure, in a stable relationship, he had marvelous colleagues, he had published a book, and he had won a "big journalism prize." And yet every morning he would wake up disappointed, missing the adrenaline of earlier years, wondering if life was passing him by—if perhaps he needed some sort of nameless change. And Rauch wondered: Isn't this sort of security precisely what we want?[1]

But for most of us, this type of security is a potent elixir, because it comes as a tangible validation of our progress. Nonacademics (wrongly) think it is about job security. It is about endorsement. It is akin to a long-term arrangement in which you and your college have shared a bond and have agreed to work toward the same goals. You will support and defend the best interests of the college; the college will support and defend your voice as an independent teacher and researcher. We often forget that the tenure arrangement is a covenant that is mutually beneficial and obligates us as well as it sets us free.

This cohort is like the best days of spring just as they merge into summer. The threat of winter is gone and you now have the energy and time to do what you want to do. It is an era of peak productivity when work goes forward without the anxiety of being assessed. Remarkably, you will even be asked to do some assessing, to look at new faculty and make decisions about their progress.

But there is also the weight of expectations. These faculty will not just join a committee, they may chair one. You are not a novice teacher; you are one of the mainstays. When the college is looking for a spokesperson, the email request comes to you. In other words, there is an *ownership* now regarding the success of the college that is tangible. People are looking to you—hoping for answers and wisdom—in a way you didn't see before. I remember serving at a church-related college

---

[1]Jonathan Rauch, "The Real Roots of Midlife Crisis," *The Atlantic*, December 2014, pp. 88-95.

that needed some insight on the biblical teaching on divorce. I took the call. On another occasion they wanted to engage the issue of the ordination of women at a national level from their national campus. The door opened again. Opportunities became abundant, and these brought as many rewards as they did risks.

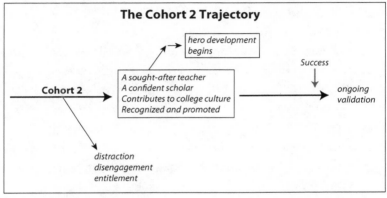

Figure 2.1. The Cohort 2 trajectory

Cohort 2 teachers have matured. They have mastered the classroom, they know how to write a grant request, they can put together a publishing proposal in a morning. The watchword is *growing confidence*. They become sought-after teachers, confident scholars and genuine contributors to the college. In recognition of these efforts, promotions often come quickly if not simultaneously with tenure. And the world of faculty development money and grants now opens in a way that it did not before. These are scholar/teachers who are comfortable in their own skin. They know what is expected of them and they know how to dispatch their duties. But they also understand that the college is a living community that requires care and support. They are committed to its health and they devote time to its well-being.

Colleges will invest remarkable amounts of time and resources in this cohort. These are the professors who will contribute to the college's reputation and represent it to the public. They will be sought out more than any cohort for leadership tasks and vision casting. The college will seek out those who are mature scholar/teachers devoted to the college's culture and who reflect its public values. A close study of those who hold major leadership positions within a faculty bears this out—and those late in Cohort 3 will often look back on their careers and say the same thing: "At this point in my life, I was doing everything and everyone wanted me to join up. In some sense, I was sought-after, valued, visible." It is interesting to study the distribution of faculty achievement awards in a college and divide them by age range. Resources pour into Cohort 2 because this is where the college's leadership looks for the heart and soul of its identity. (We will see that Cohort 3 has what we will call "legacy professors," but they are limited in number and play a very different role.)

And yet, Cohort 2 is not without its risks. The prime of summer is also filled with days laden with distractions, and the same is true with our careers—which returns us to the same theme we saw in our discussion of Cohort 1. *We can fail in any cohort if we are not self-aware.* Tenure is no guarantee of a successful career. Cohort 2 also has its stress.

One surprising study of over thirteen thousand faculty members from sixty-nine colleges by Harvard's School of Education found that this cohort (tenured with about ten years experience) was the least happy of all faculty cohorts.[2] How can this be? Kiernan Mathews, one of the directors of the program overseeing the study, tried to interpret this finding:

> Suddenly, they're teaching more, they're serving on more committees, they're even serving as department chairs—yet the criteria for promotion to full professor have nothing to do with these ac-

---

[2]S. Jasick, "Unhappy Associate Professors," *Inside Higher Education,* June 4, 2012, www .insidehighered.com/news/2012/06/04/associate-professors-less-satisfied-those-other -ranks-survey-finds. Research based at COACHE (Collaborative on Academic Careers in Higher Education) at Harvard Graduate School of Education (http://isites.harvard.edu/icb /icb.do?keyword=coache).

tivities. Many of them are like the newly tenured professor whom I recently witnessed, while setting up his laptop for a presentation, that his email client showed over 3,000 unread emails. He is highly regarded in his field, employed at an Ivy League institution, well liked by students—yet completely overwhelmed and alone.[3]

THREE TRAITS OF COHORT 2

The developmental task of Cohort 2 faculty is to become *successful.* Gone are the worries and anxieties of the novice. The classroom is familiar territory. So is the writing project. Now the aim is mastery. I remember the first time I watched a really skilled teacher at work. I had been teaching for about eight years and thought I was doing fairly well. But the truth was I only had myself as a measure of how to teach. I had never been in a college that cultivated my skills or provided a mentoring program. And then I saw him: the master teacher. His skill at presentation, his eloquence and comfort with his material, his adaptability, his emotional availability and his capacity to turn forty students into a community of learners inspired me to higher things. I had never seen anything like this before. And I wanted to imitate it.

The Cohort 2 member is skilled but must decide if he/she is willing to keep growing and let those skills evolve into something more profound. I have been inspired by faculty who take up this call and continue to grow for the balance of their careers. And I have watched others fossilize in the form they had when they were thirty-five. I recall one Cohort 2 teacher who was "finished" writing a certain class. "The Power Point is done," he reported. After a few years it became clear: each class was the same recitation of what had been taught years before. The same stories were told, the same canned explanations. He still used the film *The Matrix* as his "current" explanatory metaphor for most things. His interests and energies had gone elsewhere.

---

[3]Ibid.

I have watched numerous faculty move through these years. Three aspects of this stage of our careers are typical.

1. Teaching. Once I heard the well-known educator Parker Palmer say that what we teach is not information but ourselves. *We teach ourselves.* I had to let that settle in for a while before I understood it. Simply ask one of your students what they remember about your class one year after they take it. The experience will be sobering.

I can see an evolution in myself, and it is symbolized in a number of gestures that are so native to our trade that we barely notice. We can identify these "types" with ease because they are teaching all around us. Consider two somewhat exaggerated case studies:

Case study 1. The professor reads from her notes or speaks from a tightly organized outline. She remains behind a lectern or podium that serves as a harbor for professional safety. She might use an overhead or digital projector, but these simply give reinforcement to her control over the content that is delivered so prodigiously. Her concentration is on her notes and the effective delivery of information that she has carefully weighed and organized. You can sense she is working to get through those notes before the hour is up. She looks up occasionally, but it is a learned gesture; she sees no faces as she scans the room. At the end of the hour students may ask questions, but they are few. The room is very quiet. And when the term ends, an exam tests the students' ability to recall what has been given.

I remember watching this sort of teaching as an undergraduate, and I remember distinctly when for the first time in my life I thought about the futility of it all. For one year, I was a student at the American University of Beirut, Lebanon, and there was working on Middle East politics and Islam. I took a class that spring from a famous visiting Ivy League professor from the United States who was researching the central Asian conflicts between India and Pakistan. He came each day with a manila folder packed with lined notebook paper filled with his handwritten lecture notes. I sat up front and could see them. With unexpected animation, he read them to us. His voice went up and down—but somehow I suspected it was a trained performance. I watched his index finger glide down the page one line at a time. The students were earnest and attentive (bored students still show respect in the Middle East), and when the hour was over, he departed. He never knew us. We never knew him. He returned to Princeton. We returned to our affairs. And I wondered what we all were doing.

Case study 2. This professor builds a social community that knows how to trust itself to do the work that goes on in his classroom. Community building takes time, but he believes it is worth the time. The students come prepared because they know that they share in the ownership of the hour. And when he speaks—perhaps it is a monologue for twenty or thirty minutes—they know he is speaking from the heart. He is fully prepared—no ad hoc remarks here—but few can see the scaffolding behind his presentation. He closes the emotional and physical distance between himself and the students by where he stands and how he moves in the room. Eye contact abounds and he is emotionally present. He knows each of them by name. His explanations are driven by analogies and stories that evoke affect and reaction. He pushes them. He reassures them. He challenges them. He cajoles them. And they trust him when he says they are wrong. They are eager to talk and he provides safe space for it. They talk to one another and he releases control while still guiding quietly from the sidelines. The period zooms by, and when he says it's time to go, they look at their watches and smartphones and wonder where the hour went.

To be sure, case 1 is a negative stereotype and case 2 is an ideal. But here is the point: evolving, growing Cohort 2 faculty begin to migrate from case 1 to case 2 during these years. And when the migration is complete—when energy is focused less on the lecture notes and more on the audience—the students sense it. They hunger for it because it means they are being engaged as persons, not as recorders.

When I spend time with a new faculty member, I always give them the same assignment. I tell them to hand out index cards to all of their current students. The students then write down (anonymously) the names of five other college professors they think are absolutely outstanding in their classroom work. They can vote from what they've experienced or what they've heard on the grapevine. We then combine the cards, make a major list and look for repeating names. We even build the list so that the most frequently mentioned names are at the top. This is easy because inevitably four or five names come up again and again. I then suggest that the new faculty member go and watch each of them teach for an hour and see if they can figure out what the students admire.

Here is the discovery: these teachers will each have different styles. There is not one formula. One will use pure lecture, another seminar-style discussion, still another Socratic questions. One may be in a lab. Therefore it isn't the *methods* of teaching that make the difference. As Palmer says it: "Good teaching cannot be reduced to technique; good teaching comes from the identity and integrity of the teacher."[4] Great teachers have an uncanny capacity to be "present" in a public forum— to be "connected" not only to their students but also to the inner issues at work in their own lives.

This is why Palmer's work with teachers generally focuses on the inner landscape of the teacher's life. Successful classroom work is thus a three-legged stool: the curriculum, the students, and *who we are* in our truest selves. "Good teachers join self and subject and students in the fabric of life."[5] The great migration in teaching that takes place in Cohort 2 comes when a teacher begins to speak from his or her integrity and identity. Suddenly authenticity is born in the classroom.

A brilliant example of this evolution at work is Dr. Randy Pausch's "last lecture." Pausch was a computer science professor at Carnegie Mellon

---

[4]Parker Palmer, *The Courage to Teach: Exploring the Inner Landscape of a Teacher's Life,* 10th ed. (San Francisco: Jossey-Bass, 2007), p. 10.
[5]Ibid., p. 11.

University. At midcareer, Pausch was struck with an aggressive form of pancreatic cancer. And on September 18, 2007, he gave his "last lecture" before four hundred people (titled "Achieving Your Childhood Dreams"). Since then it has become a national phenomenon watched by over sixteen million people online (as of 2014).[6] As many said, he really didn't depart from his usual style: compelling, authentic, genuine. He will make you laugh and cheer and cry—even by seeing it on YouTube. At once we're struck with how a speaker can be so "present" even to us years later. On July 25, 2008, Pausch lost his battle with cancer, and if the message boards at the Carnegie Mellon website are any indication, he continues to inspire countless new students.

Cohort 2 faculty run the risk of teaching from habit. Patterns set in the first five years then become the template used again and again. This is understandable because of the other demands we have—every course cannot be rewritten regularly. Here I am trying to explain a paradigm shift that is possible only when the content of a course is fully mastered. *We can teach what matters instead of teaching everything.* We can engage students rather than delivering information. When Cohort 2 teachers are stuck as data deliverers, students know it immediately. As one quipped: "Their words float somewhere in front of their faces, like the balloon speech in cartoons."[7]

I remember a celebrated professor at my college telling me: "Most of the fun of teaching is when you don't entirely know what might happen during the hour." He was a historian who had mastered his subject thoroughly. No question could surprise him. And so he used the hour to invite students to join him in thinking aloud about the meaning of history instead of its details. The students knew they had to enter the class with the details mastered. I envied him, frankly, because he was having more fun than I was.

6For the video, go to Carnegie Mellon University's website (www.cmu.edu/uls/journeys/randy-pausch/index.html) or to YouTube (www.youtube.com/watch?v=ji5_MqicxSo).
7Palmer, *Courage to Teach*, p. 11.

2. Scholarship. If success and mastery characterize what it means to move through Cohort 2, there is also an evolution in our ability to work within our disciplinary specialty. Scholarship evolves from being a burden to being an enjoyment and more intensely purposeful. This evolution sometimes begins very early in a career when a certain stride is achieved and productivity almost reaches a peak. But the measure of this success is *not* in its productivity. It is in our relationship to the task. I've known tenured professors research and write with acute anxiety as if they still lived in fear of some tenure committee. This is unfortunate. Since I'm a biblical scholar (and a theologian), I value the words of the master theologian Karl Barth on this score: "The theologian who labors without joy is not a theologian at all. Sulky faces, morose thoughts and boring ways of speaking are intolerable in this science."[8] Whatever the scholarly task, it should energize us if we are succeeding. But it will be an energy not born out of fear but rather curiosity, exploration and discovery.

As I have watched successful Cohort 2 scholars, they have the same characteristics. First, they have discovered a specialty (generally in their PhD research) and have learned to hone their discipline down into a narrow aspect of the field they alone known thoroughly. I have a friend who is a marine biologist who works exclusively with a species of freshwater hydroid that is invading the Great Lakes (*hydroid Cordylophora*). I know a historian who has narrowed his field to church life and leaders in nineteenth-century England. Another Old Testament friend knows *everything* there is to know about the Egyptian/Sinai boundary deserts in the thirteenth century B.C. (when the Exodus may have happened). Another English professor is "known" for expertise on Emily Dickinson. A biologist I know works with raccoon droppings in urban settings and studies the spread of a roundworm (*Baylisascaris procyonis*) among animals and humans. Another friend is a

---

[8]Karl Barth, *Church Dogmatics*, trans. Geoffrey Bromiley (Edinburgh: T & T Clark, 1980), II/1, p. 656.

computational chemist who has explained to me what she does twice and I still don't get it (though she says it is a unique specialty).

When I was first tenured, a senior colleague told me to locate some aspect of my field and know everything there is to know about it—and get to know the main players who are contributing. As a biblical scholar my own narrowing had a careful program: Bible > New Testament > the Gospels > The Gospel of John > Historical Jesus. And soon I became a regular active member of the "John, Jesus and History Section" of the Society of Biblical Literature.

The mistake for the Cohort 2 scholar is to think that this is the time to be the "broad expert" who will write the "final word," the summative statement on the entire discipline. Very few of us will do this right now. For most in Cohort 2, that task itself will simply leave us paralyzed. If you ask one of my friends, "Well, what about the first century interests you?" his answer will be quick: Synagogues. Built before A.D. 70. Only in Galilee (N. Israel). And many of us in New Testament studies know exactly who he is.[9]

Through this specialty, we become known. It is characteristic of Cohort 2 scholars that they begin to form a network of professional friends who share their interests. They know that conference attendance is not just a luxury but a necessity in their professional development. I have a friend who attends his national conference and simply spends three days running from paper to paper to hear various lectures. I have another friend who studies the program agenda, selects his areas of expertise and growth, and makes lunch and dinner dates with friendships in his frequented academic sections. Before long, when you attend those wine receptions hosted by publishers, you actually know people there. The danger of not participating in a conference network for years is that it becomes increasingly intimidating to reenter the

---

[9]Dr. Donald Binder. See his *Into the Temple Courts: The Place of the Synagogues in the Second Temple Period* (Atlanta: The Society of Biblical Literature, 1999) and his website: www.pohick .org/sts/index.html.

arena. We get acclimatized at these things and learn how to use them.

It is this shared effort, these helpful relationships, that gives birth to new ideas, new projects and new opportunities. Last year I was working on a conference paper regarding a certain first-century pool in Jerusalem mentioned in John 5.[10] But it happened that I was traveling to Jerusalem in March for a conference. I contacted a professional friend in another university in Chicago, got linked to the custodians of the pool in Jerusalem, and when there I had all the introductions, a place to stay, and off-limits access to the under-structures of the pool itself. These happened simply through conference connections. Because I recently wrote a book on the problem of "religion" and "land" in biblical theology, another friend contacted me about joining him at a conference in Vienna next year that is looking at how early medieval tribal societies in the Mediterranean used geography and land for cultural cohesion and identity. I may go—but it is the opportunity that is valuable.

Cohort 2 scholars typically develop a rhythm to their work. In fact, if you ask them, they can almost always tell you when their most productive time is and how they protect it. They have been working now for five to eight years in their job. And their work routine is rarely haphazard since they have learned the benefits of being disciplined in their own unique way. Some have learned that late night is best. Others will build their teaching schedule to a Monday, Wednesday, Friday sequence in order to have one or two research/writing days. Most will take advantage of summers that are planned carefully in advance. Some know that the location of their work is crucial, and by now they have found a place for it. I know faculty who simply cannot write in their college offices because of interruptions and distractions. Others cannot bear the isolation of a library cubicle. The point is here: successful Cohort 2 faculty know themselves, they have built a plan for constructing a work routine, and they stick with it.

---

[10]This is the Pool of Siloam in south Jerusalem. I was comparing it with the northern Pool of Bethesda and using recent archaeological reconstructions.

Finally—and this is the most intriguing feature of this cohort—these faculty write what they want to write, not what they have to write. Their inspiration for doing what they do is not an obligation set on them from elsewhere. *They are self-motivated because the subjects they pursue spring from their own interests.* I asked a friend once if the book he was working on was tough to write. "No. It writes itself because it is something I think needs to be said." Imagine a book writing itself.

Some younger scholars research to win the approval of an imagined reviewer. Or a dean or a spouse. Others have never resolved the "core identity" validation that belongs in Cohort 1. The greatest gift in this cohort is to find some passion, some reason to write that is fueled by the joy of discovery. This is the work of the successful researcher. Again: it is not about productivity. It is about what motivates us to be productive in the first place.

I recently watched an inspiring segment on CBS's *60 Minutes* on the research work of the oceanographer Dr. Robert Ballard.[11] In 1985 he made the famous undersea discovery of the *Titanic*. In 1989 he found the battleship *USS Bismarck*. And after a long list of famous finds, in 2002 he found J. F. Kennedy's famous PT 109 naval boat near the Solomon Islands in the Pacific. Ballard has his critics, to be sure. Has he "popularized" science? Perhaps. But he argues that he must romanticize this work for the sake of funding. Despite that, it is intriguing just to read about his academic life and his work with *National Geographic*, and to watch his interviews. This man is sixty-eight. And he has retained an infectious, boyish enthusiasm for everything he does. Ballard loves his work and it shows. Whatever that spirit is, whatever he brings to his daily tasks—this taps into the very thing that makes faculty successful scholars for the rest of their lives.

3. Finding your voice. There is a final aspect of the maturing Cohort 2 professor that connects up with scholarship and teaching. It is subtle—

---

[11]www.cbsnews.com/videos/the-great-explorer-part-1-50080152/.

but it is recognizable by any who have been around it. *In some manner, these men and women have found their voice.* What do I mean?

When we begin our careers, our views, our teaching and our ideas are to some degree secondary and derivative. We make an argument and substantiate it with copious references to prove that if other scholars share this view then ours must be correct. We seem to be tentative and cautious when asserting a position—as most of us were in our PhD theses.

At some point within the life of a maturing Cohort 2 professor, something changes. Something evolves and emerges. And we begin to rely less on what others say and more on what we believe. We may work from hypotheses rather than assured results. Of course we haven't forgotten the legacy of scholarship that we've studied. But now we stand up and express a point of view—often with vigor. We write and teach out of conviction; we summarize the "accepted views" of scholarship far less in order to prove we've done our homework. In classes there is a new confidence and poise—even an interest in talking about the values at work in a subject, not only the mastery of its details (see section 1 above "Teaching").

This can be a disquieting state of affairs for some who work around us when it shows up in a predictable set of expressions. First there is a new openness to "risk." We are ready to weather criticism in a way not known before. It may be heard in an assertive comment offered publicly in a faculty meeting. It may be found in an article now published that makes waves. But the key here is that there is a new tone. We are speaking now from our convictions.

Second, this new interest in values and ethics may lead to areas of study never-before imagined. The research biologist suddenly becomes an environmentalist. The political scientist becomes an organizer of students. A philosophy professor watches the DVD *Food Inc.*, spends a year studying our food supply, and joins the ranks of the vegans—not just as a disciple, but as an evangelist. A theater professor uses a sabbatical to turn his three-legged dog into a therapy pet and writes a nationally acclaimed play called *Festus the 3-Legged Wonder Dog*. Pet therapy is now a part of his life. A theologian friend of mine has "discovered" Native American issues as an offshoot of his fascination with crosscultural theology. And some within the academy will wonder why in the world these people would risk their sterling professorial reputations on such a quixotic agenda.

My own story is typical. My work as a biblical scholar took me to Israel countless times. But in the late 1980s I began to see things I hadn't seen before. A Palestinian uprising in full swing was making work difficult there, and I was curious to see what the fuss was about. This led to ten years of "sideline exploration" into the inner workings of the Israeli-Palestine conflict. The more I saw, the more shocked I became. In 2000 another uprising erupted. In 2003 I wrote *Whose Land? Whose Promise? What Christians Are Not Being Told About the Israel-Palestine Conflict* and with it astonished a lot of my academic friends.[12] This led to numerous speaking invitations and requests for popular articles. I tried teaching a class on this subject—a colleague asked, "Is this political theology?"—and it resulted not in an esoteric academic discussion but furious debate in my own department.

The odd thing about this little detour in my career is that it introduced me to a lot of people I'd never known before. Activists. The sort of people your best friends may like to warn you about. My work in New Testament studies continued, but this little effort put me in high relief—in a way I wasn't ready for. I tried to haul this concern back to my discipline with another book *Jesus and the Land: How the New Testament Challenges Holy Land Theology*,[13] but the die was cast: in some manner I had embraced a whole lot of risk and it made some uncomfortable.

---

[12]Gary M. Burge, *Whose Land? Whose Promise? What Christians Are Not Being Told About the Israel-Palestine Conflict* (London/Cleveland: Paternoster/Pilgrim, 2003, 2013). While vilified by some, the book won two national awards: one evangelical (*Christianity Today*) and one liberal mainstream (*Christian Century*).

[13]Gary M. Burge, *Jesus and the Land: How the New Testament Challenges Holy Land Theology* (London/Grand Rapids: SPCK/Baker Academic, 2010).

Then I saw the third feature of "finding your voice." More people than you'd think will not like it. But you'll find a number of brand-new friends. And if it is a value-driven issue, people may like to argue with you and send letters or emails and blog about you and your writings. There will be a stir. Institutions that value stability and calm (and the quiet financial support of their alumni) may try to dissuade your interests. Or the theme may be prophetic and be awkward to the college's comfortable culture. Within Christian colleges, I've known faculty who advocated for issues like women in ministry, racial reconciliation, immigration reform or environmental concerns. And in some cases, the college's desire to silence them was overt.

This is one function of tenure. If we remain within the confessional boundaries of our college, this voice is protected. Nevertheless, there are consequences. Many people will tell you behind the scenes that they respect what you've done and are happy for it, but still others who are conflict-avoidant will not trust you for doing it. Finding and using your new voice will always be expensive.

My story is a parable of what many professors have told me about their own careers. Their voice emerged and the pushback was overwhelming. And they knew they were at a turning point: they either had to muster enormous energy to take on the risk or return to who they were before. Those who returned were never happy.

But for each of us this is a developmental issue. We are evolving as we should—this is an evolution that will take full flower in Cohort 3. But it is a crossroads, and not all will follow the same path.

CLASSIC RISKS IN COHORT 2

Life within Cohort 2 can come with the richest array of opportunities as well as its own unique set of risks. It too presents us with a crossroads. In Cohort 1 the crisis of security was dramatic since it was reinforced by a quest for permanence usually reflected in tenure. In Cohort 2 there are new vulnerabilities. And while they do not always lead to career failure, they nevertheless represent a significant loss that we experience within our own souls. *We have not become what we wanted to become.* We seem to have lost our way. And deep within we wonder if we are failing privately.

Such loss is devastating. In fact, it is so painful to see that we can barely admit it to ourselves. But such loss is not inevitable. If we see who we are becoming, if we recognize these pitfalls before we come upon them, they will pose little threat. I have seen a number of classic risks within this cohort.

Figure 2.2. Cohort 2—two paths

1. Discontinuing professional development. I recall once chairing the faculty committee that provided oversight for the tenure-promotion process. One midcareer professor was applying for promotion, but his department was not fully supportive, which made me look deeper into his confidential file. And there it was. Here was a faculty member who had done virtually nothing to develop himself in the nine years since he was tenured. He had attended no conferences (I asked him to be sure), he was working on no scholarship or research project, and his student evaluations were, well, less than glowing. Something was wrong and everyone working around him knew it. He met his classes and then mysteriously seemed to disappear.

These stories are among the secrets faculty hold within their ranks. We have colleagues who have disengaged from their disciplines sometime during midcareer. For some reason they are not keeping up, they do not seem interested any longer in what they teach, and if we had a moment of unfettered courage we'd like to ask them what they are doing in this profession.

I have often wondered what makes this happen. On some occasions it is a complete mystery. The professor is simply tired or dispirited or paralyzed by attempts to make headway into the discipline itself. And they have given up. On other occasions it is an academic distraction. There are faculty who become distracted by some issue that consumes them (see above, "Finding your voice"), and the moral importance of what they pursue helps them rationalize the neglect of their work. I've seen it with every sort of ethical concern: political reform, veganism, animal rights, the environment. The political science professor may join an election campaign. The musician may become a church music director. In theology there is a cross-over temptation when faculty become popular speakers or writers. Suddenly they are speaking at churches and conferences to lay audiences. "But I'm doing theology for the church" sounds meaningful and persuasive at first glance, but it may have little genuine connection with the college or our connection to our discipline. This is the flip side of "finding your voice." Rather than energizing our careers, this is activity that takes us away from our careers. And the line between the two is subtle.

Sometimes the distraction is entirely personal, with very little redeeming virtue. I remember a faculty member whose real passion was restoring old homes and vintage cars. He loved this sort of thing. But I could see by his syllabus that the framework reflected there was at least twenty years old. I knew another who loved real estate investment, but he kept telling us that he was "writing the definitive work" in his discipline. We knew better. Another colleague was completely caught up in the Parliament for the World's Religions—which might be fine except that he had ended his work as a constructive Christian theologian. I once knew a faculty member who was running a conference business out of his office (he used a hallway chair to grade papers while his hired staff worked at his desk). The distractions are endless, but they all end in the same result: they sap our energies from what we might really be doing.

One of the dilemmas that follows this problem is that colleges rarely have effective post-tenure development plans. We may have some structure in place that asks tenured faculty to report what they are doing, but generally there is very little feedback. And if a more exhaustive post-tenure report is required, we are not sure what to do with the clearly disengaged colleague.[14] Will they respond to peer pressure? Will they be inspired by career coaching? What strategies does a college possess that will renew a good colleague's waning commitments?

2. Egocentric behavior. We also know another sort of problem that is the complete reverse of "disengagement." Or perhaps it is disengagement of another sort. In this case, our colleague retreats into the private world of his/her own career. The first symptoms are subtle—fewer and fewer hours spent within the life of the college—and before long, as one friend said aloud: "I think we've seen Elvis around here more than . . ." Such colleagues may write books and articles continuously, or they may take up highly demanding roles in off-campus disciplinary organizations. They may have stellar reputations as scholars. All of the effort is directly related to their scholarship, and they may make the case that what they are doing is important (and it may be), but it is another question whether they are fulfilling the task they were hired to do as a professor.

Increasingly we suspect that they care less about the students, the department or the college—and they care more than ever about their own private career. Relationships with colleagues become strained. They seem impatient with students. When they are on campus their office door is generally closed and they don't socialize easily. They may habitually refuse all invitations to lunch.

Department chairs are not sure what to do with them. I've seen them

---

[14]The American Association for Higher Education has published a series on this topic edited by Christine Licata and Joseph Morraele. See their *Post-Tenure Review: Policies, Practices, Precautions* (Sterling, VA: Stylus Publishing, 1997); *Post-Tenure Faculty Review and Renewal: Experienced Voices* (Washington, DC: AAHE, 2004) and subsequent supplemental volumes.

show public disinterest for department meetings by doing other tasks while they sat with us. I've seen them refuse to attend "welcoming" parties for incoming young faculty because they were too busy with important things. And when they do serve on committees, their preparation and contributions are minimal. Their attendance may be spotty.

Occasionally colleges facilitate this problem—something we can explore below (see "Hero development begins"). But this problem strikes at the heart of what it means to be a college faculty member in the first place. Are we expected to pursue collegial relationships with other faculty? If there is a faculty development day, should we attend? Are we supposed to be "present" for our students and keep regular office hours? Is the well-being of the college itself important to us? If we're asked to assist a search in another department or invited to join an evaluating committee for another department, should we help out? Each of these opportunities for service requires some limits or else we would do little else. But in this case, we sense something is amiss. This person is pursuing career activities that are measurably disconnected from the college's life.

This is tragic for the college and its students to be sure. But I'd argue that it is also tragic for the faculty member. Their self-imposed research-driven isolation dissipates any commitment other faculty members have toward them. They are alone. When they announce that they are moving to another college (purportedly moving "up"), many just shrug. Students enjoy their celebrity status, but in the end, these faculty leave few lasting imprints on students' lives.

3. Institutional dissonance. There is an odd risk that can be found among faculty who have worked in a place for a number of years. They have served on committees, they know all the key administrative players by first name, and in some cases they have served longer at the college than those who supervise them. They know where the proverbial skeletons are buried, and on a few instances they may have experienced some disillusionment with those who lead. "Been there, done that" becomes a refrain heard too often. Perhaps they've seen what to them looked like hypocrisy. Or they've experienced disillusionment. Either way, cynicism has taken root and they can no longer contain it.

When I was younger I recall learning that an administrator I worked for had been giving himself loans out of the college's endowment (he was fired). In another place a friend told me how he felt when he learned that a secret salary scale was at work for some faculty that no one ever saw. I recall a midcareer colleague who discovered (it was an encounter really) that a leading trustee at his Christian college who was adept at Christian language was in reality just a rude and offensive man. That day something died in this young professor's soul. One young idealist was caught up short when she realized how power was a common currency in her college. She saw it brokered as she served on the college's personnel committee.

The question is this: When we've had a lot of these experiences, what do we do with them? The risk here is that some of us begin to pull back, not selfishly as the careerist might, but defensively because some idealism (didn't we all begin as idealists?) within us has been shattered. We once decided we would join this profession because we believed something remarkable might happen on a campus with devoted faculty and students. But now those hopes seem diminished, and perhaps the final venue for hope is in the work done in the classroom or office, not the wider college.

This experience that I call "institutional dissonance" is more widespread than any of us admit. And it defeats the creative visionary work of our careers. Imagine working for fifteen years at the Metropolitan Museum of Art in New York and one year realizing with dread and sorrow that you no longer believed in art as an important, redemptive, illuminating human exercise. Imagine remaining there because it was the only career you've ever known, the only job you think you can do—and yet, each day you do it increases the darkness that is swallowing your soul.

In all of my experiences observing this problem, I have only seen one solution: we *must* understand what is happening within us, recognize that it is toxic and find others who will not reinforce our cynicism but amend it with courage. Many of us in the academic world are idealists. We hold a *vision* for our careers. And yet that idealism gets shattered when disillusionment sets it. But it doesn't have to be either/or. We need to have the courage to find some mediating position between idealism and disillusionment, to accept some degree of imperfection in our college, our leaders, perhaps ourselves as well—and still retain that vision. But sadly—as intelligent people will—we know how to intellectualize the merits of our position and see it not as cynicism but as some sort of prophetic virtue. Then we gravitate to others who will reinforce what we've decided to believe ("See, I was right about that trustee!").

Little do we realize that healthier colleagues around us see what is going on and are keeping their distance. Our goal must be to become self-aware, to find those healthier colleagues, and by association begin to inherit their healthier outlooks.

4. Hero development begins. Faculty who have arrived at a place of security, who have wed their careers to the mission of the college, who are filled with enthusiasm for everything they do, occasionally see something that stalls their growth. They look at their peer group—all successful, growing, thriving faculty—and they see that a subset has formed. There are A-list faculty and there are B-List faculty. And they never saw it coming.

Colleges instinctively want faculty heroes. These are gifted people who can be elevated to the marquee and upon whom the hopes and ambitions of the college rest. And we should not be surprised. In virtually every career, there are artists, doctors, politicians, teachers or business leaders who are asked to step forward from the line. They carry that indefinable "something" that makes them unique. Each Sunday the *Chicago Tribune*'s business section prints photos and profiles of those leaders in the city who are "moving up." Hospitals like to highlight their finest surgeons—sometimes on billboards. *Time* magazine often prints ads showing "Best Doctors" who happen to be in your city. They even devote an entire issue to those people who are major contributors to culture and science. *Why should the academic world be different?*

Inadvertently this invisible (though very real) list surfaces. Listen carefully when someone is introduced. Or watch carefully to see who is invited to represent the college before prospective students and their parents. Introductions include descriptors such as "our best teacher," "the most sought-after prof on campus," "first among her peers," or "Wunderkind." I've heard each of these. Simply put, the college is proud of these faculty and would like to be known by what they represent. Such a reflex is as understandable as it is unavoidable.

But this can also be risky for the chosen faculty. The A-List can evolve into an "inner circle" of faculty who may sense this attention, develop attitudes of entitlement and begin to see themselves as the varsity team. I remember having lunch one day with three junior faculty. One looked across the room, saw such a gathering that was making attention-attracting noise and said, "I wonder when I'll get asked to eat at the grown-up table." The remarkable part was that everyone at our table knew exactly what she was referring to. The laughter was spontaneous and full.

Cohort 2 is where a college finds most of its public heroes. It can be unhelpful (even disastrous) to the development of these faculty who now see themselves as special. And this can have a deleterious effect on rising faculty who sense that in some manner they've been left behind. Suddenly the instinct to compete and perform—an instinct left behind in Cohort 1—reappears. Suddenly anxiety surfaces right when you thought that all anxiety was defeated with tenure. Suddenly the question of your value to the college, the students, even to yourself is put squarely in the center of your consciousness. The more a college pursues hero identification the more these risks prevail.

Faculty who feel the weight of this loss need to immediately read C. S. Lewis's brilliant little essay "The Inner Ring," which is available online.[15] This was a talk Lewis gave in 1944 at King's College, the University of London. It begins with a splendid paragraph from Tolstoy's *War and Peace* about an invisible though potent ranking within the Russian military in which captains may have more influence than generals. Lewis explains:

> Boris Dubretskoi discovers that there exist in the army two different systems or hierarchies. The one is printed in some little red book and anyone can easily read it up. It also remains constant. A general is always superior to a colonel, and a colonel to a captain. The other is not printed anywhere. Nor is it even a formally organized secret society with officers and rules which you would be told after you had been admitted. You are never formally and explicitly admitted by anyone. You discover gradually, in almost indefinable ways, that it exists and that you are outside it; and then later, perhaps, that you are inside it.

Lewis then deftly applies it to the academic careers of his listeners: "I am going to give advice. I am going to issue warnings." He says that these are perennial warnings and advice that each rising academic needs to hear. He believes that this desire to join such inner circles is a mainspring of human behavior. Then he writes, "Unless you take measures to prevent it, this desire [to enter the inner ring] is going to be one of the chief motives of your life, from the first day on which you enter your profession until the day when you are too old to care."

For some faculty, security—the deepest aim of Cohort 1—is never won with tenure. And if this is the case, a deeper exploration is needed to learn why this is not so. We may learn that we believe that who we are in essence is not good enough in our own eyes. And membership in any ring no matter how secretive or remarkable will never satisfy it.

---

[15]C. S. Lewis, "The Inner Ring," Memorial Lecture at King's College, University of London, 1944. Available on the C.S. Lewis Society of California website: www.lewissociety.org/innerring.php.

THE CLOSING OF COHORT 2

If the closing of Cohort 1 is hallmarked by a tangible sense of security, the closing of Cohort 2 is hallmarked by a sense of well-being that what you are doing, you do well. You are respected and recognized. Someone calls you with the difficult question. A dean asks you to take a role that brings satisfaction and fulfillment. You feel trusted. And though this trust may be tested when you flex new muscles and gain a new voice, still, you sense that the college continues to believe in you. You are an asset, a valued player, not expendable. You view yourself as not only competent, but successful—having mastered the twin skills of teaching and scholarship. And intuitively you understand what it is that makes the social experiment called "a college" work.

When colleges cultivate a cadre of such faculty, they do well. Colleges know this instinctively and so they cultivate and protect these professors. These are the faculty that other schools like to recruit. These are the faculty that, in many cases, our colleges are out recruiting.

Yet this is not the end of our careers. Is it not true that once we master a task, once we ascend the peak, we begin to wonder what's next? Growing, inquisitive adults do not remain static. They evolve. But here we have a problem. *Many colleges would like to see us remain precisely where we are in Cohort 2.* We are productive, teach well, have skilled relationships with students, and have honed research skills. But there is a new set of questions that marks the margin of Cohort 2 and 3. New core identity questions begin to rise. Beyond success there must be something more. And understanding it will shape how a college views its senior faculty and how those faculty ultimately see themselves.

ADDENDUM

A Financial Plan

Generally we do not like to talk about money unless the topic is how we feel underpaid. When you're a young professor at the bottom of the salary scale—with young children and a tight budget—this topic comes up regularly. When you're older with fewer financial obligations and at the top of the salary scale, this concern lessens. But there is more at stake here than a monthly paycheck. It is our long-term well-being.

In 2012 Fidelity Investments reported that its average retirement portfolio for an American worker was $72,000. Which explains why only 14 percent of American workers feel confident about their financial well-being entering retirement. According to Fidelity, 75 percent of retirees say that if they could do it over, they would have saved far, far more. But now it is too late. According to the *New York Times*, among those entering retirement in 2010, 75 percent had less than $30,000 in savings investments.[16] Middle-class workers will have it worse: 49 percent will be classified as "poor" in retirement with a food budget of $5 per day. Clearly something is wrong with this picture.

As scholars many of us live in the world of ideas and look disdainfully at the day-to-day requirements of life. But this is not an option. By the time we retire, we should try to have about eight times our annual income in savings.

I recall about twenty years ago listening to a circle of senior faculty talking about retirement. My first reaction was indifference. This didn't seem relevant to me since I was a long way from that transition. But I also knew that some of my peers were living in wholesale denial. They were saving nothing for retirement despite the fact that the college had a matching investment plan. They were walking away from "money on the table" every month. Overall, 21 percent of American workers who have access to employer-sponsored 401(k) plans choose not to participate. It's a tragedy waiting to unfold. One young scholar told me, "I can't afford to save." I told him, "You can't afford not to save."

A part of the secret is this: when it comes to investments, time is just

---

[16]Teresa Ghilarducci, "Our Ridiculous Approach to Retirement," *New York Times,* July 21, 2012, www.nytimes.com/2012/07/22/opinion/sunday/our-ridiculous-approach-to-retirement .html?_r=0.

as important as interest. Money we set aside in our thirties or forties will grow (if it is reinvested). Putting that same money to work in our sixties simply won't have the same effect. An example: if you save $5,000 per year beginning at age twenty-five and gain a 6 percent return on investment, this turns into $800,000 when you're sixty-five. If you save $5,000 per year starting at age forty with the same plan, at age sixty-five this turns into $283,000.[17] Compounding interest works like magic.

But after this particular meeting twenty years ago, a senior faculty friend in that group took me aside and told me things I'll never forget. I'm glad I listened, because it has made all the difference. He described to me how many of his same-age colleagues had not planned for retirement, were anxious about retiring and worried that when they left the college they would be financially destitute. I watched as each of them eventually retired. He was among the few who did so with financial confidence. And I knew why.

Since I was thirty I had participated in the usual academic investment program called TIAA/CREF. Thanks to my college's matching investment programs, I had set aside 12 percent for retirement for years and even diversified this into a non-TIAA/CREF program. My senior friend said this: *Each year, if you get a cost-of-living raise of, say, 3 percent (promotion years were better), march into the human resources office and increase your retirement investment by 1 percent.* He told me: You won't even feel it since you'll still get a raise—it will be just slightly smaller.

I liked the plan. I wasn't fiddling with the stock market or talking at length with financial planners who always made me nervous. I was just pushing up my savings investments incrementally. And I did it for years till I was putting away an astonishing amount each month. The surprising thing was how this portfolio grew. I continued to diversify it as I learned more about such things; but still, the difference was huge.

---

[17]Emily Brandon, "Seven Retirement Decisions that Affect the Rest of Your Life," Money, *U.S. News and World Report,* June 24, 2013, http://money.usnews.com/money/retirement /articles/2013/06/24/7-retirement-decisions-that-affect-the-rest-of-your-life.

Cohort 2 is when we need to begin thinking seriously about these matters. *Time is on our side.* But I've told you a simple secret, captured in the hallway many years ago. I now have a financial planner, and he thought it was brilliant: uncomplicated, gradual, disciplined. I've shared it with a number of friends. Many shrug with amusement. But the ones who have copied it have never regretted it.

Addendum

The Sabbatical

At first glance, sabbaticals can seem like the best perk of academic careers. Most of my extended family simply can't understand how we get these "vacations" from work. "Seriously? Your college is going to pay you to do nothing for six months?" I've learned to have an answer.

Suddenly after teaching for a number of years, the new Cohort 2 professor may be rewarded with a semester or two to do what's been neglected in her career. The exhausting effort of full-time teaching and working within the college's wider life can now pause. And other efforts, tasks long delayed, can commence.

Sabbaticals are not easy to manage. All of my colleagues have them regularly, and I've had a number as well. Stories abound about sabbaticals lost, wasted or poorly organized. Some of my friends end their sabbaticals frustrated: they often feel as if they got little done—or in some cases, focused so relentlessly on a research project that they were more tired when it was all over than when it began. This second problem has been mine. I remember spending a semester at Cambridge University (Tyndale Library) working intensely nine to five every day on a manuscript, and when it was over I was in desperate need of a vacation. However, when it was over, I had to enter another semester of teaching.

In a recent essay (2012) in the *Chronicle of Higher Education*, Domenick Scudera at Ursinus College in Pennsylvania tells us about "the true value of a sabbatical."[18] Scudera came to his first sabbatical exhausted. "All I could think about was lying around the house in my pajamas, doing some pleasure reading, cuddling with my four dogs and watching television. For the first two weeks of my sabbatical, I allowed myself that leisure time." He learned that he'd been working too hard. And the real goal of this new experience for him had to be *renewal.* He needed to be refreshed and to return to the classroom with new vigor and new ideas. However, his need for personal and professional renewal merged, thanks to his three-legged dog named Festus. It is a great article, and every first-time sabbatical faculty member needs to read it.

What are the insights few people tell us?

1. Discern what you need. Scudera is right: the first aim of this experience is to revitalize our careers so that we are energized when we return to teaching and are engaged with our disciplines in ways not known since our PhD studies. But this renewal may take on a number of facets. It is not just about working for six months in the library. It may need to be more. We may need to set personal sabbatical goals that no academic program would recognize.

I have one friend for whom physical exercise had always been a central part of her life; but her hard work at the college had ruined all her routines. Her first commitment was to rebuild her activity routines and get back in shape. Another friend wanted to revisit spiritual disciplines and so rebuild routines there that would also get her "back in shape." We are integrated people and every aspect of our health and vitality will affect our renewal. I can't imagine this, but one colleague set goals to work out every morning in our gym at 6:30 a.m., reform her diet from stem to stern, and work five or six hours each day on a research project. She'd be done in midafternoon and then devote attention to her family—things she felt she'd neglected. Her report: *the*

---

[18]Domenick Scudera, "The True Value of a Sabbatical," *The Chronicle of Higher Education,* October 3, 2012, http://chronicle.com/article/article-content/134792/.

totality of her life began to be reordered. And her research productivity increased because her overall sense of well-being had improved.

There is no formula for this. I've had colleagues who were revitalized by traveling, scheduling a long-delayed surgery, starting counseling, attending a new conference, entering a guided monastic retreat or taking a graduate class. We know the weaker parts of our lives that need strengthening, and sabbaticals are there to help us repair them. When we are whole *in the fullest sense*, we will return to our vocations new people.

2. Have a plan. Most sabbatical committees and deans require that we assemble a proposal that outlines what we want to accomplish. I have not found that this is the best place to outline personal goals. The college is chiefly interested here in academic plans. What area of research will you be pursuing? What publications will result? How will this effort contribute to your classroom work? Sometimes the plan will be modest. One sabbatical I planned to rewrite an entire class I taught each semester, build a website for it and produce PowerPoint/Keynote slides for each class period. I have found sabbatical committees to be very flexible so long as the effort directly supports the mission of the college.

However, there are insights that will help make this a success: (1) Formulate the plan early so that when the sabbatical comes you know exactly what to do. If research resources (grants, books, travel plans) are needed, these will already be in hand so you can launch your work right when the sabbatical begins. (2) Make the plan achievable. So often we want to impress the sabbatical committee with grand agendas for groundbreaking research or the major publication. And when the plan isn't completed at the end of the sabbatical, we are discouraged. This needs to be a plan that can actually be accomplished within the dates specified. (3) Work within your area of expertise, narrowing your specialty as much as possible. This means that you can capitalize on some things already written or researched. Or perhaps this is a time to pull some things out of your PhD dissertation and turn them into articles. For some, the dissertation itself may be read for an overhaul for publication.

Without a measurable plan—a real plan you believe in despite what you told the sabbatical committee—sabbaticals are almost always guaranteed to fail.

3. Locate a space. Each of us understands what we need to work most effectively. Some need the austerity and isolation of a library or lab; others require more social interaction. One colleague on sabbatical recently told me: "I think I'm going to be doing a lot of writing at Starbucks." I can't imagine it, but he certainly could. Another friend is staying for three months in a wilderness cabin in northern Wisconsin that lacks Wi-Fi. Another reserved a research cubicle in the library. Still another tried working at home but discovered that the distractions were simply enormous. I know colleagues who have obtained grants to work in research centers in Europe and at Ivy League universities. The most common theme, however, is to avoid the college office where we do our normal semester's work. Refreshment generally includes changing our venues.

The point here is that our location needs to be a part of our plan. And this particular plan needs to be organized early. There is great advantage to asking as many colleagues as possible how they organized their sabbatical and where they "set up shop." The variations are endless.

4. Manage isolation. Some colleagues disappear—literally disappear—for six months because they believe something will be compromised if they interface with their department or the college at any level during their sabbatical. Others find this isolation distressing.

I've never found this helpful. My life is woven into the life of the college, and sustaining relationships and interests there is important. For example, if I remain in my local setting and do not travel, I do not attend faculty or department meetings. And I temporarily step out of any committees I belong to. But I will make plans to have lunch weekly with colleagues, and I will attend campus events (sports, fine arts, lectures). If there is a search in progress in my disciplinary area, I may even attend the interview in order to vote. We need permission to join things we want to join. The key is knowing what things to eliminate from our involvements. Each person will have a different formula for this, but if we know ourselves we can plan what is best just for us.

5. *Travel.* If you listen carefully to colleagues, many of them step out of their college contexts dramatically. They understand that a college can be like a hermetically sealed environment where new ideas and perspectives are hard to come by. They want to dislodge old patterns of thought and expose themselves to new ways of seeing the world. When I step into a setting utterly different from my own, I begin to reframe the questions native to my discipline.

How can we do this? Of course, we may study in a foreign research university. But a more modest goal might be a teaching assignment in an unexpected place, or providing a lecture in a foreign setting. I've had colleagues do this in China, Mexico, Rwanda and the Czech Republic (just to name a few). I've taught in Egypt, Zambia and Palestine, and traveled to India, Zimbabwe and England all as a part of sabbatical plans. And in every case, I've been shaped by what I experienced there.

When is a sabbatical successful? I think that the test is fairly easy. First, do we feel a renewed sense of confidence in our scholarly work and have something to show for what we've done? It may not be a completed manuscript accepted for publication. But at least you can say your research is well underway and it will later lead to good things. Second, are we enthusiastic about returning to the classroom? For the vast majority of colleges in America, the formation of students is the first priority. Hopefully we will look forward with anticipation as we return to those relationships and have a renewed vision for what it means to be a teacher.

Cohort Three

WILL I FIND SIGNIFICANCE?

I am getting old. I find myself missing colleagues who retire faster than I can turn around, and my department keeps hiring new faculty members who are half my age and have twice the energy. My knees creak when I get up from my office chair, and I secretly ignore institutional issues that have re-circulated at least three times during my career. Yet I still love to teach, enjoy professional conferences, care deeply about my institution, and wouldn't have minded being part of several recent university wide projects.[1]

Anyone who can write a paragraph like this is solidly in Cohort 3. With a bit of whimsy Kate Sandberg at the University of Alaska/Anchorage is trying to summarize something she senses about her own development as a senior faculty member. She continues, "I have a lot of company. I'm not the only one who looks around the table at department meetings, notices my younger colleagues and thinks, 'Where did they come from?' And I'm not the only one who, on bad days, feels more and more peripheral to my institution and profession."[2]

---

[1]Kate Sandberg, "Senior Professors, Too, Sometimes Need a Helping Hand," *The Chronicle of Higher Education*, March 16, 2001, http://chronicle.com/article/Senior-Professors-Too/4861/.
[2]Ibid.

Virtually everyone who discusses the development of the senior faculty member remarks how little attention is devoted to his or her needs and interests. This is the one common feature of longitudinal studies of faculty. "Benign neglect" is the most charitable note I've read. "Ignored and tolerated" is the most severe. And this is remarkable since the number of faculty over fifty is climbing in the United States. In schools with high faculty retention rates, their number can hover between 40 and 55 percent of the faculty. Either this cohort will become a dreadful albatross in coming years or it may be discovered as an untapped resource with genuine possibilities. So much depends on how seriously colleges invest in the development of this cohort.

In a clever study of this group of senior faculty, Carole Bland and William Bergquist subtitled their book *Snow on the Roof—Fire in the Furnace.* Some college leaders (they argue) are not sure how to classify this cohort. The mistake we often make is to think that this is a cohort that is simply waiting for retirement. Or its members are defined by the completion of their careers. A number of deans have given up on them altogether thinking they are "beyond" help or development. "What's the point of thinking about faculty development for them," one leader said to me, "these faculty will never change anyway." These are men and women—rightly called senior faculty (but not as in *senior citizen*)— who are undergoing remarkable unconscious self-examination about their place in the college and their careers. Those who are thoughtful, discerning and aware of the changes at work in their lives will immediately recognize this. But as most report, they find few places in their professional life where they feel they can talk about it.

Administrative leaders often wonder what to do with this cohort for another reason. Cohort 3 faculty are typically tenured, senior, often full professors—and in some sense they seem untouchable. Or at least they are perceived to be. In one study, department chairs reported that they believed up to 30 percent of this cohort was oppositional and disconnected.[3] Sometimes they are older than the dean, and occasionally they know more about the college's institutional legacy than the president. However, this cohort has enormous vulnerabilities that put them at risk not unlike the other cohorts.

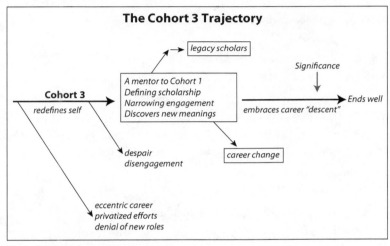

Figure 3.1. The Cohort 3 trajectory

The questions of Cohort 1 centering on *security* now are a dim memory, and it is only by building friendships with new faculty that those memories can be rekindled. The questions of Cohort 2 centering on *success* may still be at work, but as one senior faculty member told me a few years ago, "By now, I am what I am." The watchword for this cohort is *significance.* And many begin to ask what their value has been or continues to be as they serve the academy.

Many psychologists have tried to label a major personal transition that takes place at some point in later adulthood. It was Carl Jung who first used vocabulary about "the two halves of life," and this has been

[3]Robert Boice, "Primal Origins and Later Correctives for Midcareer Disillusionment," in *Developing Senior Faculty as Teachers,* ed. Martin J. Finkelstein and Mark W. LaCelle-Peterson (San Francisco: Jossey-Bass, 1993), pp. 33-41.

taken up by many. Richard Rohr describes it thus: in the first half (here, Cohorts 1 and 2) we work hard to locate security, success and "containment"—looking good to others and ourselves. These values are linked to Maslow's most basic "hierarchy of needs," and to a large degree they are centered on fear. We have anxiety that we may not survive, may fail or experience social rejection. But at some point—as every society knows—unless we move on to greater values, we become stuck in a perpetual adolescence. And this undiminished fear grows into dogmatism, fanaticism, anger and defensiveness. Always posturing, always comparing, always competing.[4] This can be true of persons just as easily as it can be true of colleges and churches.

Richard Rohr offers two insights: first, you can only see the earlier stages of life from the wider perspective offered by the later stages. This is why mature societies want to be led by the elders and not the young. The elders know the liabilities of the earlier stages. Second, each of us can only comprehend a small bit of what lies ahead in future stages. This explains, he says, "the killing of prophets" and "the marginalization of truly holy people as naïve." We have trouble comprehending them.[5]

Cohort 3 finds professors squarely in the so-called second half of life. We have spent a lifetime thus far constructing the exteriors of our houses so that they appear stable, responsible, impressive and strong. But now suddenly we realize that the interior is sparsely furnished. And our attention shifts. In fact, we care less and less about what passersby might think; we are more aware of *what we may think.* Or what God might think. If we are mindful, we are attending to deeper values and needs, rethinking if the route traveled thus far is still the course we desire. And one thing we know for sure: an ever-lengthening resume is not what we desire. In Wallace Stegner's novel *Crossing to Safety* about professorial life (he was an English professor at the

---

[4]Here I am dependent on Richard Rohr's *Falling Upward: A Spirituality for the Two Halves of Life* (San Francisco: Jossey-Bass, 2011), pp. 1-24.
[5]Ibid., p. 10.

University of Wisconsin–Madison and at Stanford), he says that what he looked back on with joy wasn't his many publications and awards—but his friends.[6] Shift noted.

Recently a colleague in classics slipped into my hands a beautiful treatise that is now over two thousand years old with the remark that these transitional anxieties are as old as ancient Rome. Cicero (Marcus Tullius Cicero) was a first-century-B.C. philosopher, orator and politician whose writings give us a remarkable window into the early Roman era. In about 44 B.C. he wrote an essay we title "On Old Age" (*Cato Maior de Senectute*), and it has become a classic text from this era. No less than Benjamin Franklin and John Adams deemed it a key to aging. The essay is a fictional dialogue between Cato the Elder and his two younger friends, explaining to them the nature of aging and why they need have no anxiety. The younger men are worried about four losses in aging: the loss of life's activities, diminishing physical vigor, the loss of physical pleasures and the anticipation of death. Cicero (or Cato) takes these on one at a time with timeless insight.[7]

I recently read Wendell Berry's wonderful novel *Jayber Crow* (2000) that touches these same themes. Its narrator (named Jayber Crow) is the barber and gravedigger of Port William, Kentucky, in the first half of the twentieth century. The novel is Jayber's attempt at the age of seventy to tell his life story and recount what now seems important to him. We meet characters from every walk of life in rural Port William: the ambitious, the lost, the violent, the loving, the sick, the wise and the foolish. We learn of Jayber's mishaps, his lost loves, his loss and discovery of community and faith, and his interpretation of life from the far end. Conversations about life and death are never ending in Jayber's barbershop, where all the men either loaf or get trimmed.

---

[6]Noted in Mary Pipher, *Another Country: Navigating the Emotional Terrain of Our Elders* (New York: Riverhead/Penguin, 2000), pp. 252-53.

[7]Many translations are available. A convenient print edition is translated by E. S. Shuckburgh, "On Old Age" (Another Leaf Press, 2012).

Reading in the paper of the death of a beautiful actress, Athey Keith said, "She has passed from the beautician to the mortician."

"What's the matter, old hoss?" said Burley Coulter to Big Ellis, who one evening stepped a little painfully through the door.

"Well, Burley," Big Ellis said, being honest, "my knees is giving me trouble."

"First your knees," Burley said, "and then your ass."

They found a certain wondrous glee in the joke of getting old and they varied it endlessly.

"Age," said River Bill Thacker toward the end of the conversation to the general effect that time, contrary to expectation, made old men out of young ones. "Age has done more for my morals than Methodism ever did."

"Well," Burley Coulter said, thinking maybe of his mother's years of dying away by bits, "some people live a long time."

Catching his tone, Bill said, "What's the matter with living a long time? It ain't going to kill you."

"No," Burley said, "Not for a long time."[8]

The book barely disguises Wendell Berry's own views (he was born in 1936), and the richly celebrated *Jayber Crow* lives, I think, as a narrative adaptation of the biblical book of Ecclesiastes. He is telling us wisdom forgotten—and wisdom that must be regained.

Another entertaining study of aging that focuses on college life can be found in Josh Radnor's brilliant independent film *Liberal Arts* (2011). Radnor wrote, directed and stars in this little gem that was filmed at Kenyon College in Ohio (his alma mater). He plays a thirty-five-year-old returning alumnus who visits his two favorite professors thirteen years after his graduation. One professor's retirement has turned into a crisis—and his favorite English professor who taught Romantic

---

[8]Wendell Berry, *Jayber Crow* (New York: Counterpoint, 2000), p. 256

English literature has become cynical about all things romantic (from books to sex). "My advice for you," she says after seducing him, "Go put some armor around that gushy little heart of yours." He then falls for a nineteen-year-old undergraduate and is forced to deal with his own aging. The script is filled with crisp dialogue, smart references to all those names we learn in college (Blake, Mozart, Marx), and student "types" we recognize immediately. And we will find ourselves in there as well. The film's final scene is a poignant, beautiful and "romantic" portrait of what it means to age.

Navigating the transitions in Cohort 3 can be challenging because it is possible to have a successful and satisfying conclusion to your career—or it is possible to fail in the necessary tasks that are before us. Here, however, there are a number of dangers, alternative paths that can threaten our success. Before we look at these closely, however, let's define the contours of what it means to live in this era of our careers.

Six Traits of Cohort 3

The developmental task of Cohort 3 scholars is identifying the value of *who they are* within the tasks that they do: to discover the task within the task. And while they are no longer worried about their security within the college—and some begin to wonder if there are still great achievements ahead of them—still there is a growing desire to know that it has all been worth it. They can sound impatient. They become impatient with scholarship that is a clever recycling of what's been said before ("What's this? Another introduction to Dickinson?" "Another commentary on Romans?"). They become impatient with efforts that will not have measurable benefits ("Who will *really* read this annual personal assessment anyway?"). They are aware of time. And they have seen how bureaucracies within colleges can generate meetings and reports, and they wonder if this is really how significant things happen. They have filled out too many "year-end reports," submitted them with student evaluations, and heard nothing in response.

One common refrain within this cohort is that feedback has all but disappeared (except for those who require discipline).

The grand mechanisms of career and life are clear by now. Validation, once sought from the college or the academy—once located externally—now *must* be located within. This is a necessary work, one that the senior professor intuits but can barely acknowledge. Younger bright faculty are rising up through the ranks. Their time has come. The college has shifted its interest to them. The existential issue is whether the senior faculty member will champion and celebrate the successes of younger colleagues or simply see them as competition.

A number of traits are characteristic of this cohort.

1. Core identity issues. In Erik Erikson's well-known stages of development, his final stages point to important issues that are deeply pertinent to Cohort 3 faculty. Erikson referred to the tension between self-absorption and what he called "generativity." Work is essential but not for the same reason. Whatever recognition will be gained has been gained. Achievements are pursued not to succeed, but to contribute something meaningful. And this is the heart of what Erikson viewed as a potential crisis. The aim of mature adulthood is to arrive at a place (he called "integrity") where we look back on our contributions and believe—truly believe—that it has all been worth it. In the absence of such belief, the mature adult is left with despair. Carl Jung said that if the older adult didn't develop such inner strength and resilience, he would become defensive, dogmatic, depressed and cynical.

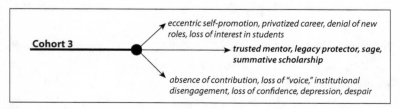

Figure 3.2. Career trajectories in the academy

This is why some faculty in this cohort are bemused by the ambitions of younger colleagues. They cannot imagine repeating the efforts they once pursued in younger years. I remember asking some younger colleagues why their foursome chose to play golf at 6:15 a.m. each week during the summer. "Why so early?" One said: "We need to hurry and get into our offices to write books and articles." The quick answer—so unaware of how it sounded—was interesting.

Sadly this decline in interest is often viewed by colleges critically: rather than understanding that a change in goals is at work, they simply see the shift in interest as a decline in productivity. But this view is anchored to an inability (or unwillingness) to understand the developmental tasks of this cohort.

The work of this cohort is to discover the significant contribution by which we want to be known and to discover the sort of person we wish to become. This effort echoes what takes place in Cohort 1 when we also worked to discover our core identity. If I have done that work—I know who I am, what I'm capable of, where my gifts lie, what my deepest interests are—then this work will correspond. If I haven't done that work in Cohort 1, then my efforts here will be virtually impossible.

Given these life-defining talents, what important tasks still lie ahead? It may be an article in the guild's most respected journal. Perhaps it is making a contribution for the general public. In many cases it is an opportunity to contribute defining scholarship that will cap a career. But almost always there is a narrowing of interest when a specialty that has been honed for twenty-five or thirty years now comes into full force. The faculty member who is still writing short book reviews or chasing dictionary articles to lengthen some list on a resume is probably missing something important. I recently received this email note: "If you write this review," one magazine editor urged, "we'll let you keep the book for free." I had to smile. This is hardly what will motivate most senior faculty members.

A friend of mine who is a psychiatrist tells me that at this stage of life, the matured adult needs to find a *mission* to keep going. "A passion?" I asked. "No. Not just a passionate interest—but an involvement, an investment, a thoughtful work that provides meaning." He describes despairing, depressed adults who come to his office and have little to live for. We should expect that this universal experience is also going to be our experience in Cohort 3. We must find a meaningful involvement that *does not* tie itself entirely to the welfare of the college. This means that we can take it with us even after we leave the college. Here is the key: if a mission is discovered (or rediscovered) then it will have the staying power to bridge us through this cohort and into retirement.

Many faculty at this stage are sadly unaware of what they want to do and do not understand their underlying anxiety about inactivity (or with Erikson, fearing meaninglessness). This is perhaps the critical role played by post-tenure reviews. The supervisor who fails to take the time to unlock a colleague's inner desire to find significance—where one can invest him- or herself and be the specialist— has missed a grand opportunity. Such reviews should never simply be a checkup to make sure a professor is still sharp. And it should not be an opportunity to enquire about retirement plans (faculty tell me that this happens regularly). It should be a chance to help these faculty find permission to pursue those things that will generate their strongest interests—because when this happens the college and its students will benefit richly.

To a certain extent I have been lucky. Because of my wife's career as a therapist, I have been exposed to psychology for a very long time. I've joked on occasion about once being in a small group comprised of five therapists, a psychiatrist and two pastors. It was a bit surreal. But this interest in psychology has permitted me to go exploring—and my own college has valued this and encouraged it. When our psychology doctoral program needed a theologian to team-teach their capstone course with a psychology professor, I was invited to take it. That was twelve years ago. I'm a New Testament scholar with no formal training in psychology, and yet this interest has flowered and found expression professionally.

2. Competency. Some have taken the view (made popular in the 1950s) that because many in this cohort are often over fifty-five, their productivity and intellectual capacities have begun to decline. Or it may sound like this: Senior faculty produce less volume (articles, books, reviews, performances) because they are experiencing a decline in energy, ideas or intellectual ability—and they are not concerned any longer about tenure and promotion. This is a common perception, and it is aligned with the idea that "all great discoveries" take place when the researcher is somewhere between thirty-five and forty-five (Cohort 2). But here we must be clear: studies of faculty productivity do not uphold that notion. There is a small correlation between age and productivity (only a 6 percent variance with younger faculty) if productivity is measured only by volume.

But the reality is more complex. To be sure, some senior faculty members do disengage from their disciplines and cease creative efforts (see below). But the reason for this is not always personal decline. This group is inconsistent. Remarkable numbers of senior faculty seek *significant scholarship* that in some manner will make a difference in their fields. This is why researchers today think that if productivity measurements are qualitative rather than quantitative, something different emerges.

There is a shift going on. This cohort is beginning to work on synthetic problems (*How do political values integrate with theological concerns?*) rather than basic questions (*How can we defend the apostolic authorship of John?*). They are pursuing larger questions, and in some cases, this is why their contributions, often longer and more complex, become career-defining contributions. Virtually every psychologist knows that aging adults begin to open the grand questions of life and meaning. Aging academics do the same.

The same is true with teaching. Several studies have shown that

interest in teaching *increases* with age.[9] Repeated studies have replicated a related result: teaching effectiveness is about the same
throughout the duration of a professor's career. Those who were effective as junior faculty continue to be effective later in life. However,
if student popularity is measured through student enrollments, the
immediate affinity students have with younger faculty will skew the
results. In evaluations *after their classroom experience*, students will
report their deep appreciation for what they found in senior faculty.
And in many cases, these scores can be far higher.

Bland and Bergquist believe that a "Pygmalion (or Rosenthal) Effect"
may be at work as well.[10] That is, self-fulfilling prophecies will shape a
senior faculty person's self-view (just as bias based on gender, race or
physical ability will). Therefore, if college leaders see senior faculty as
burned out, irrelevant and less competent—the professor will begin to
believe these very things. "Under such conditions, senior faculty will
likely become discouraged, unmotivated and distant from students,
thereby verifying the initially faulty assumptions that have been made."[11]

Some older faculty will talk about a different "tone" that they experience in their senior years when they have contact with administrative leaders. They have no memory of this happening before, and
they don't see it happening with younger colleagues. They use words
like *dismissive* and *impatient* to describe their experiences—missteps
that for younger faculty would be opportunities for formation are
handled with exasperation. Requests for grants or teaching load relief
that may be unusual—something that was praised in earlier years as
creative—now may find limited response. This is not always the case,

---

[9]Roger G. Baldwin and Robert T. Blackburn, "The Academic Career as a Developmental
Process: Implications for Higher Education," *Journal of Higher Education* 52, no. 6 (1981):
598-614, cited in Carole J. Bland and William H. Bergquist, *The Vitality of Senior Faculty
Members: Snow on the Roof—Fire in the Furnace* (Washington, DC: George Washington
University Graduate School of Education and Human Development, 1997), p. 28.
[10]Bland and Bergquist, *Vitality of Senior Faculty*, pp. 30-31.
[11]Ibid.

and I can say that in my own college this pattern is not true. But I have read and heard enough anecdotal evidence to suggest that something is afoot. Unconsciously administrators may have "reclassified" these faculty in unhelpful categories. And soon, resignation quietly floods these colleagues' souls.

But this does not have to be the case. A college culture that openly affirms and values senior faculty will see them rise to expectations. A college culture that assumes that such faculty are intransigent and hard to motivate will find them so. But there is no inherent reason to think that strong faculty who have moved successfully through Cohort 2 won't be equally successful in Cohort 3.

3. *Career change or redefinition.* Many adults change their careers in late midlife. I know some who have had two or three distinct professional jobs by the time they were sixty. For one reason or another, many academics do not feel free to follow this example. Perhaps it is the high educational investment they make; perhaps it is perceived criticism they expect. I know pastors who are in the same dilemma. The last thing you'd want to tell friends at a social gathering is that you were once a pastor for fifteen years but now are a financial planner. Or that you were once a physician but now are in social work. The follow-up questions are going to be awkward. To say you've stepped away from an academic career somehow puts in doubt the depth of your commitment to that career in the first place.

And yet I am convinced that for some, this is an ideal choice. In the end, a thoughtful career change may be a quest to pursue things postponed or denied in earlier decades.

I was talking about career change with a friend of mine who is an investment banker in downtown Chicago. He told me about the possible career moves *within* his company. In other words, if you've been stuck in the same linear career path for a long time, they could move you to another city, another role, even move you to Europe. Within a college, there are very few opportunities for this sort of movement. I know some faculty who "redefined" themselves and so reenergized their careers by becoming deans or other administrators. But this number is few. Others seek out new roles in the college heading special interest programs. But the majority are told—as many report—that the college expects them to do the same thing that they've been doing for twenty-five or thirty years and still do it with interest and skill. The problem is we experience few intra-institutional opportunities. Careers in higher education plateau. I remember raising this once in a review meeting, wondering about internal career movement. "There is nothing here like that," came the answer.

In order to find that reenergizing experience in the absence of institutional opportunities, some faculty begin to look outside the college for defining involvements. They continue to hold their jobs on the faculty but increasingly they begin to allocate more and more energies elsewhere. They are generally on a quest—they are not looking for supplemental income. The quest is about finding deeper meaning in what they do and who they are. And sadly, the college often loses out on their contributions. This becomes the source of a significant risk factor in this cohort (see below).

When I first came to Wheaton I remember meeting someone whom I admired as a teacher and a scholar. His academic contributions had helped me enormously. His presentations on most subjects were nothing short of brilliant. He was a bit eccentric, and administrators saw him as "unconventional." He was. But his classes were filled and he was a sought-after public speaker. Then I saw something I didn't expect. I watched as eventually he began organizing professional development seminars for pastors around the country. Then he published for these seminars. And next I noticed that he had part-time student workers organizing the conferences out of his faculty office.

His energies were flowing elsewhere. He had found his mission. He approached our graduate school and explored anchoring this activity at our college within the curriculum. But the door closed. Within two years his commitment to his mission was more important than his thirty-year commitment to the college. And he left.

This story had numerous other elements that don't need to be described, but the general pattern is something I've seen replicated in many, many senior faculty. A new passion was surfacing in their lives. They had linked it to their professional skills, but the college could not find room for it. And then the crisis emerges: such Cohort 3 faculty either languish in their career or follow their deeply meaningful mission.

But imagine. Imagine if that vision, that passion, had been harnessed for the curricular life of the college. I wonder how many senior faculty—the ones who have not disengaged, who continue to have a vital passion for their work—are lost every year because they sought meaning outside their academic careers.

Truthfully, perhaps another career is what is needed. In one Canadian study, 40 percent of senior faculty expressed interest in locating another career.[12] I have known medical doctors who sold their practices to find new meaning in another endeavor. I've known attorneys and pastors who have done the same. I was once speaking about this at a large church in Chicago that is filled with successful professionals and executives. A man from one of the largest tech companies in the city—a man easily in his midsixties with amazing silver hair, athletic posture and expensive business-casual attire—told me that he'd been sitting on this decision for four years. "And tonight I've decided," he said with an executive confidence that I know he used daily. He wanted to thank me for "pushing him over the edge." "I'm quitting my job. I don't need the money, the security or the recognition any more. I'm relaunching." I was impressed.

Such people are not disengaging—they are *engaging*. But their former profession is not the object of this endeavor. They have chosen another venue entirely in order to live more authentically. And hope-

---

[12]K. E. Renner, "A Survey Tool, Retrenchment Blues, and a Career Alternatives Program," *The Canadian Journal of Higher Education* 21 (1991): 115-23.

fully, with the support of family and closest friends, it becomes a life-giving, energizing moment that they never regret.

4. *The legacy scholar.* I noted in Cohort 2 ("Hero development begins") that in midcareer there are those uniquely gifted faculty whose skills of research, writing and speaking are so compelling that institutions will quickly identify them and invest in them. This is measured by the awarding of an endowed chair or release time to do research. And of course this investment facilitates more research and writing which only advances this person's identity further.

In Cohort 3 this person is sometimes viewed as a "legacy scholar." This is the unique individual who by now has a solid (and growing) publication record, is viewed outside the institution as a national expert, and is given regular acclaim by the college. In many cases, they even have their own salary scale unfettered by the constraints of public faculty salary charts.

Very few faculty will enter those ranks. And it is good to acknowledge this candidly and recognize that the majority of excellent faculty cannot do what these faculty do. It is a mark of our own maturity and inner identity when we can celebrate these older colleagues' achievements and not see them as competition, just as we should view younger successful colleagues. If they are not eccentric or self-centered (see below) they can inspire and advise other faculty and become guides to their friends who aspire to do a few of the same things.

I remember with fondness the long service of Dr. Mark Noll at Wheaton College. Mark served at Wheaton for twenty-seven years and then became the Francis A. McAnaney Professor of History at the University of Notre Dame. Mark is prolific and influential, perhaps the leading American church historian living today. In 2005 *Time* magazine listed him as one of the twenty-five most influential evangelicals in America. But for me he is a model of something important. He is the ideal legacy scholar. His humility is as inspiring as is his willingness to serve on the most modest committee. He cares about people, and many have described him as "a whole person." If you're with Mark at a Christmas party or at a faculty meeting, he really wants to know about you, your kids and your interests. Not all legacy scholars are like that.

But most of us will not experience Mark's stature. And that is okay. Everyone has different gifts. The mature Cohort 3 scholar celebrates the achievements of these scholars and is happy for them.

5. The sage. Many writers point out that Western culture is missing a vital developmental component that is shared by most cultures in the non-Western world. This is the role of the elder. We are a culture that values youth (hence the popular store Forever 21!) and rarely looks to gatherings of seniors for guidance. Seniors are embarrassed to be seniors, they are anxious about turning sixty, and they feel that their influence shrinks with each passing year. I know a leader at my college who oddly started asking me about my age every year for about five years. And then when we moved our department to a new floor and four senior faculty settled in together as office neighbors, we began to hear jokes from him about shuffleboard and "the senior section." It is no wonder that our professional world reinforces personal anxieties in this cohort.

In colleges (and most professional American settings) authority is granted by the position you hold, not by the years you've accumulated in your role. To be sure (and this is true of developing world cultures), not all elders deserve to have a leading voice. But at least in other cultures there is a category, a location, a status that the healthy senior can approach with anticipation. We have even lost our vocabulary for this role. Centuries ago a woman of wisdom was called a crone, whereas today the word is a derogatory term. A man might be a sage. In earlier cultures, a woman passed through three stages: (1) the innocent, virginal maiden; (2) the wife and mother; and (3) the elder, wise-woman, signaled by the onset of menopause (an important transition that marked the onset of wisdom). Today we have no vocabulary for any of this. J. Jill, Ann Taylor and Chico's must help the older woman remain fashionable, fresh and young. Or perhaps this is what Christian Dior meant when he spoke of his fashion designs: "My dream is to save women from nature."

Richard Rohr has done a great deal to underscore this loss and raise awareness in Christian circles. His recent book *Falling Upward: A Spirituality for the Two Halves of Life* (2011) speaks to it directly. Alex Haley once said, "The death of an old person is like the burning of a library." And similarly, the removal of wise senior adults from our culture is like locking up a library and forgetting it has books.

The reason this role has been traditionally valued is that it provides a place of significance for the senior community member. But also—and I think this is more important—it also provides guidance and wisdom for the young. Rohr likes to use the analogy of tribal societies. These elders do not kill buffalo any longer, but they know how to do it. They can teach the younger warriors the secrets of the hunt and oversee the trophies of the kill for the benefit of the tribe. Ideally, sages (both men and women) hold knowledge that must be passed down. They can tell stories that have a proverbial value. They can identify the great pitfalls. And they can evolve into caregivers for those who are younger and are struggling.

I am astonished at the number of students who now come to me *not* with questions about a class or some theoretical academic problem. They ask about life's great questions. They bring up finding a marriage partner, sexual morality, family conflicts, sexual orientation or vocational choices. Some are in despair or are depressed. Some need affirmation and positive "mirroring." Others just need to cry. Some report their victories and really want me to cheer with them and affirm them. Some raise deeply private matters that they would never discuss with younger faculty ("because it would feel weird," they say).

And that is when it occurred to me. These were students who were looking for an elder, someone they could confide in, someone who was functionally a parent or, really, a grandparent. Someone who had time for them in that quintessential way that is true of all wonderful grandparents. Someone who could listen (and not be harried), someone who was deeply empathic (and not superficial), someone whose *own issues* could be set aside for another. Someone in whom you could confide and know you would not be judged. Someone who knew about life and who had a depth of experience. Someone who could help.

If this general paradigm is true—that elders play an important role for younger members of the tribe—then something like it must be true in faculty life. If Cohort 3 faculty understand and embrace their new roles, and if the college leadership locates and promotes "elder" relationships with the "young," a mentoring program can be built that will lead to two results. First, Cohort 1 faculty will gain a significant senior friend who is not in the assessment system (particularly if they are in different departments). This will be a confidant who is still invested in his or her career and who is interested in helping junior faculty. Ideally, wisdom will be passed from one generation to another. The great legacies of college and classroom will be passed to another generation.

Second, Cohort 3 faculty will no longer be marginalized into preretirement arenas. Significant evidence suggests that regular contact with new faculty has the potential to revitalize older faculty's views of their lives and work.[13] In other words, there is genuine reciprocity here, a mentoring that in the first instance was aimed to help the young, but unexpectedly bears results for the senior faculty as well. Sadly (as I noted in Cohort 2), colleges tend to invest almost entirely in the second cohort when they are looking for mentors for the young.

Redeeming a "place" for senior faculty results in renewed confidence and positive self-regard. It will mean renewed confidence within the social world of the faculty itself and increased "ownership" in faculty life (such as faculty meeting attendance). Peripheral people rarely attend things (like faculty meetings) where they have no voice or perceive that they are not valued. The right professional atmosphere can amend that.

---

[13]Bland and Bergquist, *Vitality of Senior Faculty*, pp. 108-9.

6. Embracing descent. Developmental psychologists speak about a profound need in each of us to confront our mortality. This doesn't refer to death per se (though it might). It refers to our ability to gracefully and wisely recognize and accept that we are changing. Aging. Entering new territory. Novelist Wallace Stegner put it thus: "After sixty you are aware how vulnerable everything is, including yourself."[14] But not everyone will accept this view. I shared this notion with a faculty colleague recently, and she did not like it in the least. Soon I was receiving articles from her proclaiming how aging is artificial and unnecessary and that a constant state of vigor should be our aim. I found little in it convincing.

My first somewhat shocking introduction to this theme came from the psychologist Mary Pipher in her book *Another Country: Navigating the Emotional Terrain of our Elders* (2000). I think that Pipher probably began this writing project to catalogue what she was seeing in her elderly clients. But the book soon morphed into a sobering study of how our culture views aging, how we can view our elders sympathetically today, and what we need to be thinking about now as we look ahead. She also gave me a fresh vision for the positive role I can have as a senior adult. Her discussion of grandparents and their societal function at the end of the book is positively inspiring.

The deeper question is *how we see ourselves*. Richard Rohr is fond of talking about *embracing descent* as a countercultural gesture. He would encourage us to think about our adult lives as extended arcs. They rise gradually, peak somewhere in the middle and then descend gradually. Our lives begin and our lives end. And knowing where we are in that grand arc helps us to assume roles we otherwise might have neglected. The alternative is grim, and Rohr refers to this as the trajectory of the fool. There are those whose careers rise to a peak and then the person continues to pursue achievements, accolades and recognition like the thirty-year-old who is still collecting sports trophies for his bedroom

---

[14] Wallace Stegner, *All the Little Things* (New York: Penguin, 1967), p. 90.

wall. We know them in the faculty. Silently we worry that something is amiss with them, they have lost some dignity, or they are denying something essential about who they are becoming. He or she is the academic equivalent of the man I once knew as a neighbor who took up rollerblades at seventy-five and tried to zoom around the neighborhood.

Rohr urges us to explore the backside of this peak—to embrace it. And to use this time to recalibrate who we want to become. He points to the countless number of stories from mythology (*The Odyssey*) to the Bible (Abraham, Moses, Jesus) where the central character enters a quest that at once presents him or her with loss, tragedy, wounding, risk or danger (this is Joseph Campbell's "monomyth of the hero"). And through embracing loss, something new is born. These are the *ancient* heroes. Modern heroes simply defeat their enemies and win their trophies. Ancient heroes might die, but in their story we learn that they are the most complete, authentic and fulfilled they have ever been. Ancient heroes discover their souls. Modern heroes win fame.

The mystery of the redemption of aging is most clearly brought out in the Harvard Study of Adult Development I referred to earlier. In his full summary of this eighty-year longitudinal study, George Vaillant (*Aging Well*, 2002) forces us to read the descriptions of lives lived poorly—lives lacking generosity, wisdom, connection and "generativity" (as in Erikson). He then goes on to study perhaps the most important subjects of his books: men and women who have been closely studied—and who have aged well. A few examples are in order. Vaillant speaks of circles of generative interest that extend beyond our own lives to spouses, family, colleagues, communities, etc. As we grow, our adolescent narcissistic tendencies are transformed (among those who are growing) into increasing interest in those who are within those communities we love. When asked, "What are your dreams for the future?" virtually every person will describe dreams that do not refer to themselves but to people or programs beyond their self-interest. This leads to profound integrity, generosity, creativity and experiences of love and community unknown before.[15]

Other researchers have been intrigued with the idea of happiness. In a number of wide-ranging studies conducted by the University of Pennsylvania, Dartmouth and the University of Warwick in over 140 countries, researchers asked thousands of subjects questions such as, "All things considered, how satisfied are you as a whole with your life these days?" And the results were consistent—and labeled popularly the "U Curve." That means that when this data is correlated to age the results show surprising positive feelings among both early-stage adults (twenties, thirties) and late-stage adults (sixties, seventies). Younger people, they report, generally overestimate how happy they might be in their cohort. Mature adults consistently underestimate satisfaction. "So youth is a matter of perpetual disappointment and older adulthood is a period of pleasant surprise."[16]

In other words, there is a measurable upswing of attitude that awaits adults who age, and this can lead to remarkably fruitful and meaningful lives. Hence the "U Curve." Midlife, on the other hand, witnesses a sharp recalibration of values and identity while healthy older adults express deeper satisfaction about who they are. This is an important corrective to the dominant narrative embraced by many in the west. Healthy aging is a matter of genuine decline—but it has within it something hidden that we can anticipate with hope.

Recently I spent a week at an Episcopalian monastery in New England meeting with a senior monk named Fr. Curtis Almquist, S.S.J.E., to explore these questions. He refers to Carl Jung, T. S. Eliot, Emily Dickinson, Erik Erikson or Jean Pierre de Caussade as easily as he refers to Psalms. In one of our meetings, he offered this: The important work now is ordering our inner self (not our external world) and making peace with who we are (not what the academy or world expects). A part of that work is

---

[15]Valliant, G., *Aging Well: Surprising Guideposts to a Happier Life from the Landmark Harvard Study of Adult Development* (New York: Little/Brown, 2002).

[16]Rauch, J., "The Real Roots of Midlife Crisis," *The Atlantic*, December 2014, p. 93.

learning to let God break those things in us that once made us feel invulnerable. "Because it is in our breaking we will discover our remaking."

Fr. Almquist used an illustration from Jung. Imagine life like a rubber band—and here he stretched his arms wide in front of his flowing black habit as if a rubber band were connecting his hands. Our early adult life is about stretching, extending our reach, being visible. Then he brought his hands nearer together and moved them one above the other and I could imagine the rubber band growing smaller. In effect he said the work isn't about declining, it is about going deeper, concentrating, thinking about matters of significance, finding deep satisfaction in things that have been on your mind for decades.

"But what about publishing another book?" I asked.

"For whom are you writing it?" he asked me.

Descent—rightly understood—brings with it freedom and authenticity. As one monastic proverb describes, freedom is found in the context of limitation—which is why Richard Rohr titled his recent book *Falling Upward*. Descent is a fall, but it is a good fall because within this descent very good things come. As Mary Pipher puts it, this is not about growing old, it is about growing whole.[17] "Very truly I tell you, unless a kernel of wheat falls to the ground and dies, it remains only a single seed. But if it dies, it produces many seeds" (Jn 12:24). This, as Fr. Almquist likes to say, is the deepest level of the Paschal Mystery. *True life is found on the other side of death.*

For the professor this shows up in greater levels of authenticity in the classroom and with colleagues because we are teaching from our center, not from a persona we've built. Quickly students will intuit that we are at peace with ourselves; we've explored some way to integrate what we believe and who we are, and they will yearn to tap that mystery for themselves. When this happens, by the grace of God, a sage may just possibly be born. This is what is so completely appealing about

---

[17]Pipher, *Another Country*.

Wendell Berry's dozens of books to countless readers. Through the eyes of people like Jayber Crow we glimpse a man who has found peace.

CLASSIC RISKS IN COHORT 3

In many respects, the features of Cohort 3 I have just explored also have their shadow sides. By denying or avoiding developmental tasks in this cohort, we immediately find ourselves at risk of failing to become the person we'd like to become. When I was in seminary, I studied with one of the most remarkable senior faculty I'll ever meet. Dr. Everett Harrison was easily in his late sixties when I knew him (he lived into his nineties). And he was beloved. Our classes with him were about what was important in life, and we knew it. We were listening to Fuller Seminary's sage. Students came to hear him pray. Others simply wanted time alone with him. He was patient, kind, unimpressed by big-name scholarship and content in who he was. He was centered, and we coveted his serenity. After he retired, an entire community of graduate students continued to meet with them. Later in life, Fuller students cared for him. And upon each, he left his mark. I was one of them. Here I am thirty-five years later writing about him.

But I also remember other senior faculty in a variety of places where I've worked and studied. And some were not what they could have been. I'll never forget a panel that Fuller Seminary organized for first-year students. Dr. Harrison was there—as were four others. The question was put to them: *What makes a healthy spiritual and personal life?* Dr. Harrison spoke first and his words were calm, eloquent, assured. The others sounded apprehensive. The final professor wept openly before all of us and said he'd probably failed. It was one of those moments you don't forget. We were witnessing a broken man grieving the state of his life.[18]

---

[18]This was George Eldon Ladd, whose theological brilliance was matched by the utter tragedy of the later years of his life. See the remarkable biography by John D'Elia, *A Place at the Table: George Eldon Ladd and the Rehabilitation of Evangelical Scholarship in America* (New York: Oxford University Press, 2008).

Some of us know that a mysterious transition is beginning when we enter Cohort 3. But we don't know why and we don't understand it. This is why, when I turned sixty, I went on a guided New England retreat at a monastery. After some research, I had three options: Iona in west Scotland (Presbyterian), Emery House in northern Massachusetts (Episcopalian) and Christ in the Desert in New Mexico (Catholic). I chose the monastery at Emery House for one reason: to listen to myself in silence and to listen to a senior monk who was (in my view) a sage.

So the question remains: What are the pitfalls that can defeat us in this era of life? Let's explore a few.

1. *Disengagement and disinterest.* If it is true that there is restlessness in our souls—or as my monastery counselor in New England put it, something luring us elsewhere—there is the possibility that we will begin to lose interest in our work. We have already seen this in Cohort 2, and it can reappear here. Academic subjects that once inspired and motivated us now seem mundane and boring. We stop reading the important books. We no longer visit the periodical section of the library to look at the latest journal publications. Academic conferences seem less than they were and we no longer imagine presenting a paper. We don't improve our syllabi. In the remarkable (and uncelebrated) indie film *The Visitor* (2007), the first scene opens with a senior professor in New England, recently widowed, filled with despair, using Wite-Out to change the dates on his aging syllabus before he photocopies it for another semester. When a graduate student walks in and sees him doing this, we feel the pain of his embarrassment because he knows what he used to be and realizes what he has become. *The Visitor* has one subject: a professor's redemption.

I mentioned above ("Career change or redefinition") that these passages are natural. But this is another problem. Because every faculty member is bright and gifted, rather than finding renewing ways to reengage our disciplines, we may go far afield to satisfy ourselves. I've known professors who devoted themselves to real estate investment, photography, the stock market, antique auto repair and missions tourism. Not only were their students neglected, but these faculty were not doing what their college genuinely needed them to do. This can only end poorly.

What can we do to refocus ourselves? First, we can discover a way that our discipline intersects with a subject that is new and refreshing: we can explore the more integrative dimensions of our work because it is these values that we yearn for most deeply. We need to look on the margins. Sometimes this will take us into organizations that are off-campus and only minimally related to our immediate work in the classroom. But what it will do is reinvigorate us, and this renewing experience will often help us reengage our careers. I've seen geologists begin working with students on village well development in Africa. I've seen philosophers begin teaching about medieval philosophy in Florence, Italy, after developing a travel program there. I've seen political scientists awakened by international justice issues such as prisoner treatment and conflict resolution. I have a friend whose house burned down one year and the next year was divorced by his wife. He now spends one semester each year in Jerusalem leading his college's off-campus program in the Middle East. He worked hard to find a fresh venue for himself.

Since my specialty is the Gospels (and their cultural setting in Galilee), I decided to work two seasons at archaeological sites in Galilee (Bethsaida, Sepphoris). I took eight students each time. We had our own van, and we drove all over Galilee on weekends. It was fun and renewing. And I developed skills I didn't have before. I've also had a longstanding interest in political science and the Israel-Palestine conflict. It doesn't take long to learn that for many conservative Christians, theology intersects with this area directly—and this led to conference and publishing involvements (and not a few controversies). But I think on a deeper level what I was doing unconsciously in both cases was looking for professionally related activities that would energize me, that didn't take me too far afield and that brought me back into my career: New Testament studies.

In post-tenure evaluations of senior faculty, imagine if deans and department chairs helped senior faculty explore such options. Imagine a wise dean leading such a meeting and surprising a senior faculty member with these sentences: "Here is a $1200 grant. I want you to go out and find something that you'd dream about doing, something that might change you. Bring me the proposal. I'm sure we'll both love it. And the money is yours." For the professor, it is a redemptive possibility. For the college, it is a small investment in recovering a valued faculty member.

Second, we can renew our love for our college or university. Members of Cohort 3 have often already explored most roles within faculty governance and many report that when, late in their careers, they try to participate again, there is sometimes limited opportunity or welcome. Nevertheless, every one of our colleges has a wide variety of programs that we can join, and it is up to us to find them and explore them. In my case, I sought out our international internship program that places about thirty students each year somewhere around the globe for six months. I found I really liked its leaders, I believed deeply in the values of the program, and I gravitated to the students who were in the program. I joined their advisory committee, became a mentor to one student each year, and every summer I fly somewhere around the world to meet up with them where they are working. Last year it was Nicaragua. Before that, India. The year before that it was Egypt, and before that, Jordan. We have programs connecting athletic teams with individual faculty (I'm involved with the women's basketball team) and student clubs (I'm inclined to the justice-oriented gatherings). But the point is, I've found new ways to connect with my school, ways that help me enjoy what I'm doing in unexpected ways. And all of it corrects the professional disengagement that may begin to rise.

Third, we have to realize that our main work is with students. *When we lose our love of students, almost all is lost.* Therefore by working hard to reenter student life (attend any activity and let students see you there; begin scheduling lunch with students you like) we are reminded that we work not to please the academy but to serve the growth of our students. For years now I have shamelessly taken photos of each of my students on the first week of class. I load them into my computer, label them with their names and make a spreadsheet out of them. And within weeks I memorize their first names. What does this do? Initially it impresses the students who remark that few of the faculty know their names. But for me, it bonds me to them. They are persons. I know them now, and my classes are about relationships, not information transmission.

2. Self-absorption, reclusive behavior. Some senior faculty disappear into their offices and rarely emerge. In some rare cases, they have become eccentric, finding value only in what they publish. In other cases, they have simply privatized their careers. Without realizing it, some become almost reclusive or occasionally abrasive in social gatherings. Students find them awkward to be with; anecdotal stories begin to circulate about insensitive things said in class; they miss faculty meetings or department meetings. Sometimes when they are there, well, *they are not really there.* They may sit and grade papers or read email discreetly on their portable devices. Or they may simply disengage mentally.

I remember once having a well-published colleague who was so abrasive that I had not talked to him in years. Neither had my friends. One day he was using the copier before me and I thought I'd give it a try. "So tell me how your semester is going," I said somewhat cautiously. "Fine. And have you read Thielman's application of realized eschatology to the problem of Paul and the law yet?" I had not, I confessed. He looked unhappy and left me to do my copying. It was awful. And I'm sure he had no idea how he was pushing people away.

Another story: I remember joining three or four colleagues for lunch over the years and regularly trying to recruit the same person again and again to join us. No luck. He stayed in his office, alone, rarely coming out.

For some faculty, just appearing in our wonderful faculty dining room recalls feelings of high school cafeterias. I know. I've tried coaxing them.

There is some research that suggests that for a few senior faculty, acute anxiety based in insecurity leads to compensatory behavior. Some faculty can even exhibit signs of paranoia and fear that in some manner others are planning things that will harm them. Conversations in the hall that don't include them are viewed with suspicion. A dean appearing in the department makes them apprehensive. Some respond aggressively; others retreat and disappear. I have enormous compassion for these colleagues (although I must confess that I'm less tolerant of those who harm their fellow faculty members). Nevertheless, I still see that what they are doing springs from a deep place of brokenness and sadness. Where they are living must be a very lonely place.

The first sign of this problem is isolating behavior, when the routines of the normal workday are suddenly reduced to walking to class, returning from class and remaining in your office, often with the door closed. We often dress it up with thoughts about how much writing we need to do or how interruptions are keeping us from real work. But in our deepest selves, we know something else is happening. And it may be frightening just to admit it—frightening because we don't know where it is coming from and we're not sure what to do about it.

In some rare cases, this isolation can be symptomatic of depression, particularly among those in their sixties. And rarely (but it must be said) this despair can be dangerous, leading some to end their lives. This is not an imaginary possibility. It is real. In the last ten years, suicide rates for American adults in their fifties and sixties has increased by 50 percent for both males and females, according to the Centers for Disease Control and Prevention.[19] And while there are no major studies that can

---

[19]For a summary, see B. Bahrampour, "Baby Boomers Are Killing Themselves at an Alarming Rate, Raising Question: Why?" *Washington Post,* June 3, 2013, available online: www.washingtonpost .com. The male suicide rate is four times higher than the female. Statistical increases: males, ages 50–54, 20.6 suicides per 100,000 population (1999); 30.7/100,000 (2010). For females ages 60–64 the same trend follows: 4.4/100,000 (1999); 7.0/100,000 (2010). See the American Foundation for

get at the root of what is causing this, most speculate that this generation can live with a deep sense of despair that the idealism (or existential fulfillment or high expectations) they had sought in their formative years has not been realized. Add to this many years of economic stress, and despair can become toxic. However, just knowing about this, knowing that there are such dark paths, can help inoculate us from their pull. And then we can take steps to make a course correction. Isolation and the loss of friendship may be an early sign.

Without trusted friendships, we become stagnant and something in us begins to die. Anything we do to step away from this dangerous place can help us. It may be locating one same-age colleague we trust, or initiating something social (coffee, lunch, golf). It may be requesting that our classes are across campus in another building so that we have to walk to get there. Just the effort of walking, mixing, saying hi to passing strangers begins to soften us. Our campus has chapel three times each week. Just attending once each week might make a difference. What we do is less important than that we do something. We step out. We take a risk because we know that if we don't, things for us will only get worse. The happiness we once knew will only get harder and harder to recover.

I have a very good friend who is single and as a social scientist has researched friendship formation, how it works and what it does for us. And here is the thing: she is a living example of what she teaches. I see her scoring basketball games at the bench, joining a freshman mentoring program, having lunches and dinners with colleagues, working out in the gym, being active in her church, even organizing weekend activities (like go-cart racing, museum trips, bike rides) for any comers. She isn't perfect—she'll tell you that, but she's aware of trying to be healthy. She refuses to be isolated.

A good friend is a treasure when we are not doing well. And when they come to us and speak gently of what they see—and even if they

---

the Prevention of Suicide (www.afsp.org) and the CDC (www.cdc.gov/violenceprevention/pdf /Suicide-DataSheet-a.pdf).

take the risk of suggesting that we "talk with someone professional"—we need to be open and receptive. That one person may be the one lifeline that helps us find ourselves again.

3. *Technology anxiety.* For some Cohort 3 faculty, the fast pace of technological advancement is wearying. Their careers began when typing on an IBM Selectric typewriter (complete with automatic character correction) was a luxury. There were no computers. Today we cannot imagine our careers without them. For the most part, Cohort 3 faculty have kept up. But for some, the continual shifts in how we use the web or the latest software has become a labor rather than an opportunity to improve work or discover new things. *Cloud? What cloud?* we wonder.

I remember a faculty development seminar where a young, chipper professor distributed "clickers" to each of us and demonstrated through a slick web interface on a screen that we could all register our opinions to questions by clicking A, B, C or D on our devices (you can do the same thing with a smartphone app). So we tried it. Immediately a bar graph (fed by an immediately built online database) appeared on the screen. "Now imagine," she said with a chipper voice, "We could start doing this in our classes!"

I looked across my table at a Cohort 3 prof who rolled his eyes, moaned and put his forehead on his neatly folded hands resting in front of him. We heard him murmur: "And why do we want to know students' opinions about everything anyway?" The rest of us knew him well, knew this was just like him, and we broke up laughing.

We all know that there is a basic level of computer literacy that is required of us. We have to keep up to some extent. But just because new software is invented or a new web application appears, *it doesn't mean we have to adopt it.* Just because we can do something with technology doesn't mean we ought to do it. But when we feel insecure about these things, we often don't feel confident to object to them lest we be named among the luddites. Those of us who are comfortable with computers reject "clicker invitations" all the time—not because they intimidate us but because we feel they are a distraction or inefficient or unnecessary.

Remember that education is a human enterprise. It is a communal activity. And there is no replacement for the craft of a skilled teacher leading his or her students through complicated educational terrain. No software program will ever replace that.

4. Role confusion with students. One of the deeper joys of Cohort 3 is learning that a new role is before us. Students will come to us for reasons that may surprise us. Above I noted the surprising number of times now that students will come to me seeking advice about matters completely unrelated to the college. It is important to remember that they are not coming looking for a new friend. They are seeking a friendly adult who will remain an adult.

The role confusion I describe here is the faculty member who never grows up. He or she is the perpetual adolescent professor: joining intramural games, wearing outfits shared with nineteen-year-olds, socializing in student circles and interacting with students as if they were one of them. In a word, these faculty have forgotten their boundaries. One professor I knew decorated his office with piles of sports equipment—just so you knew he was still on teams. Another had students over to watch *Twilight* DVDs on his home theater. I see this and wonder at the hidden things that must be driving such behavior.

I remember once being invited to an engagement party by one of my favorite students. I showed up to a campus house packed with about fifty students and no other faculty while the newly engaged told stories about their first date, first kiss, most embarrassing moment and other sundry matters. A lot of the subjects had not-so-subtle sexual themes, and the crowd cheered them on. I would have made my escape but there was no back door. I was in the wrong place and I knew it. The cultural pressure of our society is to appear perpetually young or at least cool and to imitate those who are half our age. Students secretly talk about such faculty, and we don't want to be their subjects.

Cohort 3 presents us with an invitation to live out who we really are.

I believe it is because of the many broken families and communities we live in today that many of my students are desperate to find mature adults in whom they can confide. The mantle requires that we live with dignity, wisdom, restraint and patience. No one of us will be perfect with these, but we strive to realize our virtues as best we can.

THE CLOSING OF COHORT 3

Cohort 3 ends with retirement. And the perennial question (sometimes avoided discreetly) is when this decision ought to be made. Just for the record, this decision is personal and, since 1994, a college or university cannot impose mandatory retirement.

We are fortunate to live in a country where retirement is not required at sixty-five. My PhD mentor in Great Britain was forced by his university to retire when he was at the peak of his career. It seemed absurd. He was drawing scores of PhD research students right up till he was in his midsixties. What were they thinking?

Many factors weigh into the retirement decision: finances, health (mental and physical), job satisfaction, general vitality, interest and other opportunities that may be calling us elsewhere. The calculus in the decision always has to take these into account and is never easy. For some, early retirement might be best. Others are effective till they are seventy or more.

What do I hear from my retired friends? I'll include some notes below (see the addendum). Above all they have always desired that retirement would be something (a) that they control and (b) that they may anticipate with happiness. We've thankfully left behind a world where retirement meant gardening and golf. Perhaps it is the legacy of the baby boomers who are swamping this demographic now that settled assumptions will all be challenged. My retired friends, the ones I desire to imitate, each look for significant meaning in what they do. They are not at rest. They are continuing to pursue lives of curiosity, contribution and self-discovery. When you meet with them *they are always interesting.* They talk about more than their grandchildren. It may be the latest play they've seen, the book they're reading, the board they've joined or the organization they are active in. One friend of mine volunteers in a refugee camp in Palestine every summer. Many have the resources for personal investment that they never had before.

As faculty we should end well. As professors, we have been part of one of the most important institutions in our culture. We should look at our contributions—the silent ones when we helped students, the larger ones when we gave speeches or performances or wrote books—and we should feel satisfied. Of course we will think of things not done and things not said and feel some disappointment. Or we may experience regrets about books or articles we wish could be rewritten or positions we no longer hold but yet somehow came to define us. In such cases, we may need to exercise generosity with ourselves. This may be a time of needed grace, a time when we measure ourselves not by what we didn't get done, but by what we did.

ADDENDUM

Retirement

I mentioned earlier that a long time ago a wise senior faculty member gave me some important advice about investing (see Cohort 2, "Addendum: A Financial Plan"). He was a sage in the best sense of the word, and I learned to listen to him. So throughout my career I have followed this instruction: always listen to colleagues who are at least ten years older than you. When you are forty, talk to those in their fifties. When you are sixty, find former faculty in their seventies. Ask them what you should expect, what has changed for them and how they might have done things differently. If you are sincere, they will tell you things you will hear nowhere else.

I have been listening to retired faculty for a few years now. Some retired just a couple of years ago, most are in their seventies, a few are in their eighties. Some are very happy and fulfilled; others are not. But consistently these are the themes that return again and again.

1. Retire before you have to retire. Again and again, senior faculty will talk about teachers who "should have retired" but didn't. In a word, their effectiveness was simply slipping away. And everyone knew it. I know one poignant story about a professor who happened to overhear a colleague's lecture and heard troublesome incoherence. They were very old friends. And together they met and talked gently about what this might mean. We heard a retirement announcement three months later.

Having to endure such a conversation of course hurts our dignity. But the worse part about it is that we are no longer able to bring real vitality to the life we will have after we retire. Retiring before you have to retire means students and colleagues will miss you, they will not breathe a sigh of relief. There will be a celebration, and you will feel fit to get on with something new and interesting. But what is true about effectiveness is doubly true about health. We want to bring our healthiest selves into retirement.

2. Make sure your financial plan works. Retirement "poverty" is increasingly going to be a feature of the coming decades. Social Security benefits are constantly in jeopardy and Medicare may be scaled back. Retired faculty always bring this topic up first when I talk to them because they have seen friends retire not knowing what they will have to live on. One friend I know had to sell his house when he retired, and he only realized this after he left.

An astounding number of faculty live blissfully unaware of their financial well-being. My own financial advisor (a Wheaton graduate from many years ago) has intimated stories of ill preparation among professors that are tragic. A surprising number of us do not put away money for retirement (even when there is matching money from our employer on the table). I honestly do not understand this. Faculty are smart, thoughtful and know how to do research. Human Resources departments can almost always help us with a financial advisor. (If we are using the ubiquitous TIAA/CREF or Fidelity companies, they will supply one for free.)

3. Have a plan and a purpose. I have been warned about this more times than I can count. When we retire, we cannot think that what gave us meaning before retirement will continue to do so after we retire. We may not be teaching—and writing or speaking opportunities may dry up. A busy, productive professional life must be replaced by something meaningful or else we will find ourselves slipping into lethargy and despair.

Such plans have to be made early, preferably before we retire. It may be joining a board, an editorial role at a publication, a volunteer activity or perhaps part-time teaching in a different venue. But we must discover something that is purposeful. We are naive to think that the fame or significance we enjoy on campus today will remain. I recently attended the retirement reception of a good friend (who is devoting his remaining years to higher education in Congo!). He told me as we hugged without spilling our glasses of the usual orange "retirement punch": "Remember, Gary, at a college once you retire the college moves on and you will be quickly forgotten." I didn't want to hear it, but I knew he was right.

4. Keep your friends and skip the move to Florida. Or Arizona. I didn't see this one coming. But retired faculty will tell endless stories about people who sold their home, fled the northern winters and moved to Florida or Arizona. And then they spent the next ten years wishing they were back home again with their old friends. It is a curious fact that friendship formation is much more difficult as we age. And friendships are critical to our well-being. Those relationships we have cultivated for years are precious beyond measure. Recreating them in a distant place will be hard, harder than we imagine.

A good friend of mine just returned from his sabbatical. I knew he was thinking about retirement. And I also knew he was thinking about selling his house and buying a very cool cabin in another state (read:

a lake, a mountain and a large porch for his dog). He tested this by renting a place in that general area. Last month he returned and gave me his report: the move would be too remote; he's keeping his local home and friends; and he's not ready to retire. He said the question isn't where to retire. The question is "with whom" you will retire.

I was not surprised by his awareness of his own needs. He's a psychologist. But the exploratory trip is now in my notes and is certainly something I'm going to imitate some day.

SELECT BIBLIOGRAPHY

Baldwin, Roger G., and Robert T. Blackburn. "The Academic Career as a Developmental Process." *Journal of Higher Education* 52, no. 6 (1981): 588-614.

Benne, Robert. *Quality with Soul: How Six Premier Colleges and Universities Keep Faith with Their Religious Traditions.* Grand Rapids: Eerdmans, 2001.

Bland, Carole J., and William H. Bergquist. *The Vitality of Senior Faculty Members: Snow on the Roof—Fire in the Furnace.* The ASHE-ERIC Higher Education Report 25:7. Washington, DC: The George Washington University Graduate School of Education and Human Development, 1997.

Boice, Robert. "Faculty Development Via Field Programs for Middle-Aged Disillusioned Faculty." *Research in Higher Education* 25 (1986): 115-35.

———. "New Faculty as Teachers." *Journal of Higher Education* 62, no. 2 (1991): 150-73.

———. *The New Faculty Member.* San Francisco: Jossey-Bass, 1992.

Boyer, Ernest L. *Scholarship Reconsidered: Priorities for the Professoriate.* Princeton, NJ: Carnegie Foundation for the Advancement of Teaching, 1990.

Camblin, Lanthan D., Jr., and Joseph A. Steger. "Rethinking Faculty Development." *Higher Education* 39 (2000): 1-18.

Filene, Peter. *The Joy of Teaching: A Practical Guide for New College Instructors.* Chapel Hill: University of North Carolina Press, 2005.

Finkelstein, Martin J. *The American Academic Profession.* Columbus: Ohio State University Press, 1984.

Finkelstein, Martin J., and Mark W. LaCelle-Peterson, eds. *Developing Senior Faculty as Teachers.* San Francisco: Jossey-Bass, 1993.

Greenspan, Stanley I., and George H. Pollock. *The Course of Life.* 7 vols. Madison, CT: International Universities Press, 1989–1991.

Hughes, R. T. *The Vocation of a Christian Scholar: How Christian Faith Can Sustain the Life of the Mind.* Grand Rapids: Eerdmans, 2005.

Kindlon, D., and M. Thompson. *Raising Cain: Protecting the Emotional Life of Boys.* New York: Random House, 1999.

Lawrence, J. H., and R. T. Blackburn. "Aging and the Quality of Job Performance." *Review of Educational Research* 56, no. 3 (1986): 265-90.

Levinson, Daniel J. *The Seasons of a Man's Life.* New York: Ballantine Books, 1978.

———. *The Seasons of a Woman's Life.* New York: Ballantine Books, 1986.

Litfin, Duane. *Conceiving the Christian College.* Grand Rapids: Eerdmans, 2004.

McCabe, Linda L., and Edward R. B. McCabe. *How to Succeed in Academics.* San Diego: Academic, 2000.

Palmer, Parker. *The Courage to Teach: Exploring the Inner Landscape of a Teacher's Life.* San Francisco: Jossey-Bass, 2007.

———. *Let Your Life Speak: Listening for the Voice of Vocation.* San Francisco: Jossey-Bass, 2000.

Pipher, Mary. *Another Country: Navigating the Emotional Terrain of Our Elders.* New York: Riverhead/Penguin, 2000.

Pollack, William. *Real Boys: Rescuing Our Sons from the Myths of Boyhood.* New York: Holt, 1998.

Sadler, D. Royce. *Managing Your Academic Career: Strategies for Success.* St. Leonards, NSW: Allen & Unwin, 2000.

Sandberg, Kate. "Senior Professors, Too, Sometimes Need a Helping Hand." *The Chronicle of Higher Education*, March 16, 2001; http://chronicle.com /article/Senior-Professors-Too/4861/.

Schwehn, M. R. *Exiles from Eden: Religion and the Academic Vocation in America*. New York: Oxford University Press, 1993.

Simon, Caroline J. *Mentoring for Mission: Nurturing New Faculty at Church-Related Colleges*. Grand Rapids: Eerdmans, 2003.

Stegner, Wallace. *Crossing to Safety*. New York: Random House, 1987.

Tournier, Paul. *Learning to Grow Old*. Louisville/London: Westminster Press/SCM, 1972; repr. New York: Harper & Row, 1983.

Viorst, Judith. *Necessary Losses: The Loves, Illusions, Dependencies, and Impossible Expectations That All of Us Have to Give Up in Order to Grow*. New York: Random House, 1987.

SUBJECT INDEX

Finding the Textbook You Need

The IVP Academic Textbook Selector
is an online tool for instantly finding the IVP books
suitable for over 250 courses across 24 disciplines.

ivpacademic.com